The
EWA
MATAYA
Pool
Guide

The EWA MATAYA Pool Guide

EWA MATAYA
with BOB BROWN

AVON BOOKS  NEW YORK

The rules on pages 120–132 are excerpted from *Billiards: The Official Rules & Records Book* and are reprinted by permission of the Billiard Congress of America.

"Annie" cartoons created by Vicki Paski; illustrations by Ken Simonsen.

THE EWA MATAYA POOL GUIDE is an original publication of Avon Books. This work has never before appeared in book form.

AVON BOOKS
A division of
The Hearst Corporation
1350 Avenue of the Americas
New York, New York 10019

Copyright © 1995 by Ewa Mataya
Cover photo courtesy of Antonin Kratochvil
Interior photographs by Tim Dell © 1994
Published by arrangement with the author
Library of Congress Catalog Card Number: 94-23367
ISBN: 0-380-77645-6

Library of Congress Cataloging in Publication Data:

Mataya, Ewa.
   The Ewa Mataya pool guide / Ewa Mataya with Bob Brown.
      p.   cm.
1. Pool (Game) I. Brown, Bob, 1940–   . II. Title.
GV891.M38 1995   94-23367
794.7'3 — dc20   CIP

First Avon Books Trade Printing: March 1995

AVON TRADEMARK REG. U.S. PAT. OFF. AND IN OTHER COUNTRIES, MARCA REGISTRADA, HECHO EN U.S.A.

Printed in the U.S.A.

Q 10 9 8 7 6 5 4 3 2

*To Mitchell and Nikki,
the loves of my life*

Contents

Introduction

$\mathscr{I}$t is one of those remarkable moments that defines the attraction of sports. An overflow crowd surrounding four brilliantly lighted tables on the floor of the Biltmore Hotel's grand ballroom in New York has just seen Loree Jon Jones make a Woman's Professional Billiards Association tournament record run of sixty-four balls. And this is just an opening round game in the United States Open. It just doesn't get much better than this.

Oh?

Just twelve minutes later, attention in this vast, rococo room has shifted to one of the three remaining tables in play. On that table Ewa Mataya, the woman whose 54 ball record Jones has just broken, is starting her own sustained run. Tall, slim, and striking in an immaculately tailored black evening suit, Mataya is the number-one-ranked woman player in the world. Her record will not be relinquished without a fight.

As she moves about the table, Mataya's green eyes laser-scan the balls. Angles and patterns are registered, subsequent lies are plotted, defensive options are weighed. There is an economy of motion and time in her movements, but no indication of impatience.

Many of the spectators have a personal rooting interest in this drama, having met Mataya earlier in the evening when she brought her game to match sharpness on a practice table set up in the lobby

1

adjacent to the great, gilded room in which the matches are played. Mataya chose not to warm up in isolation, like a boxer in the solitude of a dressing room, but on a table purposely set up to provide fans with access to the players.

There is no question that Mataya is a crowd favorite. She is a handsome woman. But appearance alone does not account for her appeal. The conversation she carries on as she warms up has a sincerity that both attracts and holds the audience.

It is an opinionated crowd, made up almost equally of women and men. As the practice session goes on, Mataya smiles and shrugs at the occasional shot that does not drop. She talks easily to the growing crowd, in a voice that is rich in tone and crisp, with every syllable fully enunciated. It is a voice that actresses could emulate. And it is all the more remarkable because English is Mataya's second language. Swedish is her native tongue, but it is difficult to detect any trace of an accent or jarring grammatical constructions as she converses in English. Nor is her speech overly formal or stilted; Mataya makes liberal use of American idioms.

Laughter frequently punctuates her banter, and it is appreciated. Someone in the gallery questions Mataya's shot selection. As usual, if she acknowledges criticism at all, it is with a toss of her long light brown hair and a shrug. The critic is easily disarmed.

Knowledgeable spectators, and those who have witnessed Mataya's warm-up sessions before, realize that she is not out here in the lobby of a hotel, before a major match, just to sink balls and impress her fans. This is a warm-up session, not an exhibition. She is honing herself for the coming competition, reviewing fundamentals, testing equipment, evaluating conditions.

Now inside the ballroom with her record so recently broken, Mataya knows that she must continue to adapt herself to changing conditions. Here, under the intense lights, on a different table from the one on which she practiced only minutes ago, surrounded by an anxious audience generating waves of heat and humidity, the game she will play is, again, totally new. Tactics must change, balls will react in new ways, Mataya must adjust.

It is nothing new to her. Mataya analyzes. She makes subtle changes, revises her strategies, and chooses her shots. She also must factor in the response of her own mind and nervous system to the fact that—for now, at least—she is the *ex*–record holder.

Tap, click, ker-thunk. As the standing-room-only crowd collectively holds its breath, Mataya continues the run. Balls disappear into pockets. New racks are made.

It is, for the most part, a knowledgeable audience. As patterns appear in the layouts of the balls, it becomes more and more obvious that Mataya is "in stroke."

Tap, click, ker-thunk. Racks are run and whole new strategies are formed as the balls redistribute themselves.

Tap, click, ker-thunk. Although three of the four tables are still in play, the crowd on the ballroom floor—which now includes the new record holder, Jones, who is seated in the front row—can focus only on the table on which Mataya is building her run. In the balcony overhead, spectators edge close to the railing.

Tap, click, ker-thunk. Time after time, the tall figure bends low over the table, the cue is brought slowly back, then smoothly forward. Ker-thunk!

Tap, click, ker-thunk. Mataya is unhurried as she stalks the table. Off to the side, the scoreboard shows her nearing fifty balls made.

Tap, click, ker-thunk. Now Jones's record is in sight. Mataya banks a ball cross sides. It is as difficult a shot as can be found on a pool table. Mataya not only makes it cleanly, she establishes position to run out the remaining balls in this rack.

Mataya allows herself a quick smile of satisfaction—and relief—which the crowd takes as permission to exhale in audible unison. They share the sense of accomplishment.

Tap, click, ker-thunk.

Tap, click . . .

This is a tournament, after all, and play on the other tables goes on even as Mataya closes in on Jones's minutes-old mark. Yet it is clear that the other players are as caught up in the drama as are the spectators.

And no one is more riveted than Cathy Vanover, Mataya's opponent, who sits watching this extraordinary run that will surely send her to defeat.

Tap, click, ker-thunk. Mataya drops down over the cue again, chin tight to the shaft, exactly as it has been on every previous open shot.

Tap, click, ker-thunk.

Ball number sixty-five falls. The record is Mataya's once again. Balls continue to fall. Finally . . .

Tap, click . . .

The incredible run comes to a halt. Mataya has sunk sixty-eight straight balls. She has held the table for more than twenty tension-building minutes. Vanover, in almost stunned appreciation, shakes Mataya's hand.

Although it is hard to think that there are not mixed emotions across the room, in the front row of the gallery, Jones applauds enthusiastically and smiles broadly. This, after all, is what pool—real *pool*—is all about.

Mataya, too, smiles. And she gives an acknowledging wave to the audience.

It had been a champion's response to a challenge. Mataya that evening was Reggie Jackson at the plate in a World Series . . . Joe Montana in the pocket in the final seconds of a Super Bowl . . . Jack Nicklaus ninety yards from the pin at the Masters . . . Jackie Joyner-Kersee readying for the 3,000 in the Olympic Pentathlon.

Like those champions, Mataya possesses the rare combination of training, discipline, concentration, competitiveness, and talent that defines an athlete who has the ability to rise to an occasion. It is a combination that made her the number one player in the world.

She also is one of the most sought-after coaches in the world. Just as her tournament record is no accident, Mataya's success as a teacher is no coincidence. She has been an avid and disciplined student of the game since she was a teenager playing in the scholastic pool leagues of her native Sweden.

It is in part because of this academic background that Mataya is uniquely equipped to improve *any* player's game—from rank beginners to tournament-level experts.

Mataya has created a comprehensive and proven teaching system that needs little more proof of its effectiveness than her own success.

On the following pages you can learn from Ewa Mataya—at your own pace. Learn how to develop the strong fundamentals. How to judge and correct those fundamentals should your game suddenly "go off" (and it happens to almost everyone sometime). How to select the right equipment. What to look for in forming strategy. How to develop your mental gamesmanship.

Plus Mataya gives you instructions on how to perform dazzling exhibition shots. It is her commitment that just because you are becoming an expert, the fun should not go out of the game. And mastering pool will be fun. Guaranteed.

—Bob Brown

Preface

*I*t might surprise you to learn that I studied pool in school. Not after school, in school. As a subject.

Do I hear someone saying "What kind of school would teach kids to play pool?"

Hmm. I see your point. Nowadays, as the mother of a school-age child and living in North Carolina, it does sound a bit unusual, even to me.

Maybe the first thing we should do is to take some time to fill you in on my background. It has a lot to do with both my becoming the number-one-ranked woman player in the world and my respect for the sport—and with why I have written this book.

I was born in Sweden. My father, Lennart, owned a factory that produced window blinds and awnings in a small town about 120 miles from Stockholm. I was introduced to pool the same way most kids are—socially. When I was about fourteen my older brother Mats and his friend used to play quite a bit of pool at a local billiard room. I went along with them a few times with my friend Nina. At first, Nina and I only watched, but after a couple of times at the club, we wanted to play. I fell in love with the game almost from the second I picked up a cue stick.

Up until that moment I played lots of sports throughout school: basketball, hockey, skiing, soccer (I was the goalie on our school

5

team that finished eighth in the nationals). But from then on, pool became my main sport.

Both my father, Lennart, and my mother, Ingbritt, were very happy that I had found something I really liked. Especially that it was pool. The sport is very highly regarded in Sweden because it involves so much strategy and tactical planning along with physical ability and training. The clubs where pool is played are very nice and modern. Similar to golf clubs, almost all of them have a teaching pro.

Looking back on it, I can see that my parents were instrumental in nurturing my progress. Together with the billiard club I belonged to, they helped to buy my first cue stick and gave me money so that I could play in tournaments and make the trips they required.

Part of the curriculum at schools in Sweden is "free choice." It is similar in concept to electives in the United States. Free choice allows high school students to pick from a wide variety of courses and activities and get credit for them. Our school did not have pool tables on the premises—although many Swedish schools do—but when I saw that pool was one of the listed activities I naturally chose it for my free choice course.

That was when I really started to learn and understand the game. Most of the lesson time was spent on the fundamentals—holding the cue properly, bridges, and other essentials. I was fortunate that I had a good natural stroke, but, believe me, I wasn't some fourteen-year-old prodigy who had "world champion" stamped on her forehead from day one.

The late Bjorn Johnson played at the same club where the course was held. We all called him "China." He was a former Swedish and European champion. But more than that, he was very generous with his time. He began giving me lessons. China showed me how to think in patterns and how to make the game easy on myself. When I began to see how China went about analyzing the game and how much the inner mind came into play, I just thought, "Wow! I don't know anything." But I knew I wanted to learn.

I had been playing only a few months when I was selected to go to a tournament. I was fourteen at the time. It was the first national tournament for women ever. I finished fourth.

My club paid much of my expenses to most tournaments, and over the next several months I had some good finishes and I got to travel—

not just in Sweden, but to other European countries as well. I graduated from high school when I was sixteen and then started college. But I think even then I was committed to playing pool as a career. I had already won the Swedish championships in 1981. After I won the European championship in Bern, Switzerland, in 1981, the head of the Swedish Billiard Association asked me if I could go to the United States and play in the World Championships in New York City. I talked it over with my parents, and they agreed that I should make the trip.

I was seventeen and loved New York. I also met Jim Mataya, a professional pool player who was entered in the World Championships, and I fell in love with him. I called my parents and told them I was going to stay in the United States and get married. Of course they were surprised, but I've always had a mind of my own and they understood.

Jim and I lived in Michigan. At that time, the women's pro tour was not very well organized. It was difficult to earn a living just by playing pool, so I also tried my luck as a fashion model, mostly in New York and Detroit. Then, in 1985, my daughter Nikki was born.

The three of us—me, Nikki, and Jim—went to tournaments together. It was a very hectic sort of life and I did not do all that well. Things were also changing in women's pool. The tour was becoming more lucrative, which meant that the competition was getting better just at the time when my concentration was at a low point. But when Nikki started going to school full-time, I was able to practice more steadily and my game began to come together again. Having a practice partner in neighbor, best friend, and top female pro Vicki Paski didn't hurt any either.

Then the breakthrough came, in 1988, when I was signed on as a player representative for Brunswick Billiards. Besides being the leading table manufacturers in the world, Brunswick has long been active in supporting women's pool by sponsoring professional tournaments and their involvement in furthering amateur billiards here in the United States and abroad. For me it was the boost I needed. Two years later, in 1990, I won five tournaments and made enough final rounds in several other tournaments to become the number-one-ranked woman player in the world. Since then, I've traveled throughout the world playing in tournaments, giving exhibitions, and acting as a spokesperson for the Brunswick Billiards Corporation, which also gives me a lot of support so that I can continue to "go for it."

And, in a way, my life has come full circle in that now it is Ewa Mataya who is teaching people how to play pool.

It has come full circle in another way as well. Jim and I divorced, and Nikki and I have moved to North Carolina, where I have remarried, to Mitchell Laurance. Even though I have obligations all over the world, I make sure my schedule includes plenty of time to be with my family and to be there with Nikki as she is growing up. I remember the support my parents gave me and how much it counted in my own career, and I want to offer the same thing to my daughter.

Ewa Mataya's Tournament Victories

1981   Swedish 9-Ball Championship, Sweden
1981   Swedish 14.1 Championship, Sweden
1981   European 14.1 Championship, Switzerland
1983   Clyde Childress Memorial World 9-Ball
1984   Old Milwaukee Team Cup Champion
1984   Clyde Childress Memorial World 9-Ball
1987   Brunswick Team Challenge Championship
1988   International 9-Ball Championship, Japan
1988   World 8-Ball Championship
1988   U.S. Open Championship
1990   Cleveland Spring Open
1990   East Coast 9-Ball Classic
1990   Sands Regent Open
1990   Cleveland Fall Classic
1990   Rocket City Invitational
1991   U.S. Open Championship
1991   WPBA National Championship
1994   World 9-Ball Champion

A Note from Ewa

Since no one can learn all there is to know about the game of billiards, or even close to everything, in a single lifetime, reading books and studying the game through magazine like *Pool & Billiard Magazine* and *Billiard Digest* is a great shortcut to expanding your knowledge.

If you are fortunate enough to live in the same town as — or have the opportunity to study under — teaching legends such as Jimmy Carras or Dorothy Wise, maybe reading should be secondary. But for most of us, hitting the books is the fastest and surest way to improve.

I have played pool now for sixteen years, read most of the available books, spent hours and hours on the practice table, and played in thousands of tournament games. I'm excited about being able to share with you the knowledge I have picked up along the way.

That's not to say I don't still have a lot to learn myself. And recapping most of what I know has been a help to me, too. Going back to the basics every once in a while is a healthy thing for us all. I have also included information that very definitely is for the advanced player. Such information is clearly indicated. I do that not because I don't want novices to learn it but because I don't want beginning players to become frustrated when they can't perform the techniques I am suggesting. Pool is a tough game, but it should not be a frustrating one.

I also would like to take this opportunity to thank and acknowledge the people who have helped me with my game, my life, and this book. And I apologize to everyone not specifically mentioned, but you know who you are....

Thanks to my mother and father, Ingbritt and Lennart; my brother Mats; Nina Kristrom; Bjorn "China" Johnson; Leif "Gneten" Johansson; Jim Mataya; Vicki and Bob Paski; Jim Bakula, Pat Kelly, and Kathleen Scanlan at Brunswick Billiards; Shari Stauch and Harold Simonsen; the guys at Pockets; everyone at Mothers; my co-author and friend Bob Brown; and all the other great male and female professional players on the tour whom I have had the opportunity to play and watch.

The Game —
An Overview

One of the most attractive—and intriguing—aspects of pool is that it has a "dual personality." That makes it unique among ball games. Harold Simonsen, a friend of mine and the publisher of *Pool & Billiard* magazine, puts his finger on it when he says: Pool is the only sport in which you are in control of your immediate destiny—as in bowling or in golf—yet you are competing directly against another player at all times—as in tennis.

Pool looks deceptively simple because it is a "passive ball" game. What you do determines the result of a shot. If you line up the shot properly, and you hit the ball properly, you will make the shot. It's as straightforward as that. I've recently taken up golf, another passive sport game. The ball might be up on a tee, or lying on a fairway, or even buried in the rough, but it's up to you to make the shot. The ball isn't going to move until you hit it.

Tennis, or any of the racket sports, certainly seems more difficult. In those "active ball" games, you must hit an object moving toward you, or at least toward your side of the net. And it can be loaded with all types of spin and pace. Pool is also unlike baseball, where you, as

11

the batter, must determine the trajectory and spin of a ball pitched at you from sixty feet six inches away. Depending on the talent of the pitcher, the ball can curve or skid, or can even drop suddenly in a manner that seemingly defies physics. Just ask Michael Jordan what it's like to try to hit a major league curveball.

So if all these tricky things are what pool is not, does that mean it is an easy game? Not on your life. It's fun. It's easy to understand. It's inexpensive. It's played by people of all ages. But easy? No. If it were "easy," it would not have been able to maintain a popularity that extends over at least three centuries.

The secret of pool's success is that in compensation for being a "passive ball" game, it also makes extraordinary demands on the player. There is almost no margin for error. You must hit that passive ball just about perfectly. Every time. If a tennis player merely returns the ball over the net, he or she has succeeded—or at least has not lost ground. If a batter merely connects with a pitch and hits the ball to a spot that no one can reach before it touches the ground, that's a major triumph! And if he can do that only three out of ten times, he's sure to be earning a seven-figure salary. In pool, the demand is that you hit the cue ball exactly right—not just connect with it—every time.

And your perfect shot on the cue ball is only the first step. The cue ball then has to travel along a path that will cause it to hit another ball, also in precisely the right spot, that will send the second ball on a path into one of the table's six pockets. Pool allows you all the time you need to hit a ball that is sitting perfectly still—you can figure out the angles, judge the force you need to use, determine the English you want—but in return, it demands a degree of accuracy and control that no other game requires. If you make a good shot only three out of ten times in pool, you probably won't get an invitation to play another game—except, maybe on the table in your best friend's basement.

But that isn't the end of it. Pool also demands that you play against an opponent at all times. Pool is not like golf, where you "play" opponents simply in the sense that you keep score while each goes his own way hitting separate balls for nine or eighteen holes. Let's say I shot a 72 (I wish), and the people I "played against" shot a 78, a 96, and a 115, all for the same eighteen holes. What I shot had no effect on the scores of the other three players but because I did not have to make as many shots I won the round.

Now, take pool. You and your opponent are playing the same cue ball, and in some games the same object ball. So if you miss a shot, you lose your turn to your opponent. Moreover, if you had set up the following shot, you probably gave your opponent an easy shot ... in fact, you gave your opponent your easy next shot. At all times, you must not only play position for yourself, you must play position against your opponent. It's very much like chess, where you are consciously and constantly planning offensive and defensive strategies simultaneously.

Because of this unique combination of precise physical demands coupled with constantly changing tactical situations, a game of pool is always fresh and fascinating. That's why everyone, from youngsters to senior citizens, can enjoy it equally. The more evenly matched the players are—on any level—the more exciting the game becomes.

There is still one more attractive aspect to pool: you don't have to listen to people making excuses. I say that with tongue in cheek, but it's true that when things go wrong in pool, there is only one person to blame. There's no wacky spin on the ball that made you mishit it, no wind gusts, not even any lucky bounces. Nothing. You do your thing and you get to take the credit ... or the blame. In that manner, it is a wonderfully "honest" sport.

Now it is time to get you into this equation. We have been talking solely about the game, but you are the one who will be playing it. You should be aware of your own potential and limitations. There are determinants as to what that potential might be:

1. **Basic eye-hand coordination.** No big surprise here. I'm not going to kid you, not everyone can become a top tournament pro. Just as in basketball, there are Michael Jordans and there are people who can't get past *O* in a game of H-O-R-S-E. Just remember that anyone, at almost any level, can improve his or her stroke mechanics. It may require an overhaul in stance for a beginner, or it may mean a subtle shift in balance for a pro, but with analysis and knowledge, everyone can improve.

2. **Desire.** Let the psychologists debate whether the root of winning is "a will to defeat an opponent" or "a fear of losing." The level of play you can bring yourself to comes from how much time you re-

ally want to put into it. How do you reach your next goal? Practice is the key. There is no substitute for quality table time. And fortunately, pool practice never gets to be drudgery because pool is a game of infinite variety.

But desire also means that you are always on the lookout to know more about the game: learning from teaching pros, from observation of other players, and from studying books and videos.

3.   Concentration. You will find this point being repeated time and time again in this book, but it is a point worth restating: Pool is a game of control. And it only follows that the control must begin with you. Seeing the shots, stroke mechanics, finding the patterns: all those elements must come together if you are going to be successful. They will do so only through concentration. And not just when you are at the table. It helps to concentrate even when your opponent is shooting. You should keep playing the game in your mind, even when someone else has the table.

Like stroke mechanics, concentration is an art that can be learned and improved upon. I certainly don't have anything against the idea of somebody looking into meditation as a way to heighten the ability to concentrate. At least, if you're serious about the game, try to play each practice session as if it were the World Championships. (That way, when you finally do get there, you'll be right at home!!)

Equipment

CUE STICKS

$\mathcal{P}$ool is not an equipment-intensive sport, but that doesn't mean you can be casual about the gear. Almost all of us begin playing with a one-piece house cue. Nice, serviceable, and efficient. If you know what to look for in choosing a house cue, you will have the foundation for when the time comes to buy your own cue.

Most cues fall in the 18-to-21-ounce range with an overall length of 57 to 58 inches and a diameter at the tip of 12 to 13½ millimeters. (I play with a 19-ounce Brunswick cue that is 57 inches long with a 12¾ millimeter tip.)

If a house cue stick is of the general weight and length that you like, you can check to determine if it is reasonably straight. Roll it on the table surface. It should roll smoothly and not bounce or jump.

Certainly, if you play more than a couple of times a year, it pays to buy your own cue. A $50 to $75 cue should be sufficient. *Well-made*, well-balanced cues are not difficult to find in that range. Over time, as your game improves and you find yourself playing more and more, you may want to consider a more expensive cue. Remember, a cue that costs $150 to $300 may last for years. That's

15

an amount that, at sale prices, might get you a beginner set of golf irons—leaving the woods, putter, maybe a wedge or two, a bag, and shoes still to buy before you can tee off.

There is one final thing to mention about cues. Treat them as you would any fine wooden instrument. That means they should be cleaned. Forget waxes, aerosol "dusters," and the like. If you own a cue and it has some sort of buildup on it, you might want to try to clean it with one of the commercial cue stick cleaners. But there's nothing wrong with plain soap and water. This is wood, however, so use the minimum amount of water possible.

For cleaning the plastic ferrule, you can use "whitening" toothpaste, which will get the dirt and grease off without scratching the finish. A few light strokes with a soft rag loaded with toothpaste is all you should ever need. And, of course, keep your custom cue stick in its case to minimize the swelling and shrinking caused by temperature and humidity.

The tip demands some particular care. You want to keep the tip shaped—it should be about the shape of a nickel. A tip scuffer, fine file, sandpaper, and "Tip Tapper" helps in this aspect of cue maintenance. The tip must be replaced when it becomes too flat.

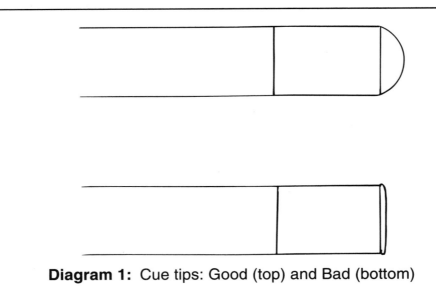

Diagram 1: Cue tips: Good (top) and Bad (bottom)

SPECIALTY CUE STICKS

To keep with our golf analogy, you might want to have a few extra clubs in your bag. One to think about is a "break cue." Its purpose is to deliver the maximum amount of power on a break. That's only a partial justification. The real value in a break cue is that it saves your playing cue stick from possible damage. Generally the break is the most forceful stroke you will make and there is no sense in risking the cue tip or the ferrule.

And then there is the "jump cue," a stick that is gaining popularity along with the game of nine ball. Jump cues are almost a necessity for pros. Frankly, you should learn to make jump shots with your own cue before going to this specialty stick. Jump cues are very short and their weight is distributed to make them comfortable with the butt end elevated to an extreme. Some players get away with simply unscrewing their cues and using only the shafts on jump shots.

CLOTHING

Comfort and common sense should guide you. Nothing binding. Nothing crimping. And nothing too loose. You don't need the distraction of a loose, floppy sleeve getting in the way of your bridge hand—particularly on those tight-to-a-rail shots—any more than you need a too-tight sleeve preventing you from stretching out on a long shot.

Both the men's and women's pro tours have specific dress codes depending on the type of tournament. You don't have to worry about that. Given a choice, men seem to favor casual clothes, although Willie Mosconi was always a fashion plate. For women, a pair of well-tailored slacks and a blouse or top along with casual or low-heeled shoes with nonslip soles is fine for most occasions. Be aware, however, that big rings and loose bracelets—particularly on the bridge hand—are not a good idea.

POWDER, PAPER, AND GLOVES

The cue stick must pass between your bridge fingers as smoothly as possible. The idea of drying moist hands with cornstarch or talc or any of the brand-name powders is a good one. But too much powder on your hands can quickly cause a buildup on the cue stick. In other words, you are aggravating the very problem you are hoping to solve.

In order to keep the cue stick smooth, it can be refinished with ultra-fine sandpaper. I use number 600 paper, which has an almost undetectable grain. It takes just a light touch-up to keep my cue stick smooth at all times.

Recently gloves have come on the scene. I don't use them, but if you are worried about excessive moisture on your hands, try one.

TABLES

Much of the time you have no choice as to which table you play on. Nevertheless, the table is perhaps the most important piece of equipment you will be dealing with. Fortunately, there are ways to understand any table and to make that understanding work to improve your game.

This holds true for beginners as well as experts. While the experts are at a level where they are constantly evaluating table conditions, even over the course of a single game, to see what adjustments they must make, novices cannot be expected to be so sophisticated. But novices should be able to recognize enough about table conditions, too, so that their confidence is not destroyed when shots seem to go unexpectedly awry. If you don't recognize the vagaries of a table, you might blame a bad shot on aiming or stroke mechanics, when the actual cause is the condition of the table itself.

Here are two points to remember:

1. No two tables play the same.
2. The same table may not play the same on different days.

Even in this day of automation and standardization, pool tables require a lot of individual craftsmanship in their construction. Some tables are simply better made than others. They also incorporate—to varying degrees—natural materials (wood, rubber, slate, fabric), and Mother Nature never uses the exact same recipe twice. It's those variables that explain why no two tables will play exactly alike.

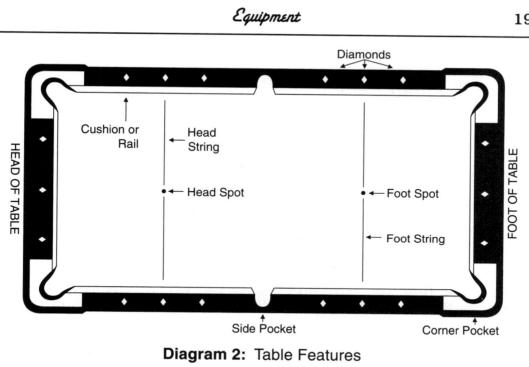

Diagram 2: Table Features

Some of the differences will be clearly apparent. Professional tournament tables, for instance, are a uniform four and a half feet wide by nine feet long. But home tables, and even commercial tables, come in a variety of sizes, generally maintaining a length-to-width ratio of two to one.

A more subtle cause of variance among tables is the cloth that covers the playing surface. The "felt," as it is often called, can come in a variety of textures. At one end of the spectrum there is heavily napped cloth, with a high percentage of wool. You can stroke this type of cloth and easily feel the heavy grain of the weave. So-called no-nap cloth is at the other extreme. It is a durable nylon-based fabric that has a barely discernible amount of nap and grain. In between these extremes is a variety of textures for table cloths—and, of course, wear will cause any fabric to change its playing characteristics.

Just as there are some tennis players who do well on slow surfaces, such as the grass at Wimbledon, there are others who thrive on hard courts, such as those at the U.S. Open. You should know how to "read" every surface and how to adjust your play. You don't see Steffi

Graf taking a pass on Wimbledon just because she likes a faster surface better any more than I would pass on an event because it was not played on Brunswick tables.

A table's cushions are perhaps the most difficult items to evaluate. The height at which they are mounted determines where they impact a ball, which in turn can affect the amount of spin on the ball when it comes off the rail.

And because rails are usually made of natural rubber there are unavoidable differences in resiliency.

In addition, the nature of a rail will change as conditions in a room change. For instance, the higher the humidity gets, the shorter the angle the ball comes off on will be. For instance, a ball that you might anticipate will come off the rail at a 45 degree angle will come off at a tighter angle — say, 42 degrees. That's a significant difference. Conversely, the drier the atmosphere, the "longer" the rails will play. The ball will come off at a more open angle — that is, the same ball you expected to come off the rail at 45 degrees will come off *maybe* at 47 degrees.

In tournament play, changes in the size of the spectator gallery can cause big differences in the amount of heat and humidity in a room within minutes. The pros have to be constantly on the alert as to how the rails are playing. In most recreational situations the ambient conditions may not change, so once you evaluate how the rails are playing on a given day, they should stay that way for at least the duration of a game.

3

Fundamentals

STANCE

*O*nly golf allows the player the luxury that pool does in terms of planting your feet to establish the most stable platform from which to hit a ball that is stock-still. Watch someone like Jack Nicklaus prepare to tee off and you'll understand how importantly he regards this aspect of golf. As he shuffles and wiggles and settles into place, he is looking for balance and maximum stability in his stance. And you can be sure that Nicklaus takes all the time he needs to get that stance exactly right.

But he just has to hit one ball. Because pool requires that the player hit a cue ball precisely so that it will, in turn, strike an object ball with similar accuracy, there is an even higher premium placed on balance and stability. That vital combination will not come together on a consistent basis unless you are comfortable. Nor will you find it if you do not adopt exactly the same stance whenever it's possible.

Mary Kenniston, one of the top female players, and I were discussing how we taught ourselves to take a consistent stance and we discovered that each of us had hit upon the same technique. We

Ewa's Pool Stance

"walk into the shot." This method virtually guarantees that you will develop a stable and unvarying stance.

This is the routine:

1. Stand back from the table and visualize the shot.

2. Take one *normal* step toward the cue ball with your left foot, so that when you extend your bridge hand (do not stretch out too far) it is about six to eight inches behind the cue ball.

3. Bend down over the cue stick until you feel most comfortable to aim the shot.

To help me draw a comparison with another sport, I will call on my friend Bengt "Jonas" Jonasson. He has done quite a bit of boxing, another sport in which balance is extremely important. Even though a boxer is constantly moving, he must maintain stability to throw a punch. Jonasson envisions that he is standing in an imaginary square. His feet are at diagonal corners of the box, so that he will have the maximum leverage and stability when he throws his punch. There is much the same need in pool, only you must make a stroke with a cue stick.

You can imagine yourself standing in the imaginary box on an extension of the aiming line between the cue ball and the object ball (in boxing, that would be the path on which your fist will travel when you throw the punch). In this way, your stance enhances not only your balance but your aiming as well.

I'm five-foot-ten and right-handed. When I take my stance, the distance between my lead foot (my left foot) and my trailing foot is approximately eighteen to twenty-four inches, depending on where the cue ball is on the table. I cite these measurements and distances only as a guideline to help you custom-tailor your stance to your dimensions.

A lot of the pro players, myself included, flex the lead leg just slightly at the knee while keeping the back leg almost locked. Other players prefer to flex—just slightly—both knees. Either style is fine, but I notice that players who flex both knees often have a tendency to spring up when they stroke the ball. If you sense that happening on your follow-through, flex only your front leg and the problem just may correct itself. Other than that, there is no hard-and-fast rule about bending your legs. The goal is to make yourself both comfortable and balanced, and you can use whatever works best.

By establishing the right balance point, you also will be adopting a stance that prevents you from extending too much. I mean that literally—stretching way out looks dramatic but if you do this you run the risk of losing some control over the cue stick (you are working with a longer lever, which magnifies any errors you may make in aiming or in executing your stroke). Save yourself for the times when you *have* to stretch in order to reach a shot. There's no sense in handicapping and tiring yourself by looking as if you are performing aerobic exercises at the same time you are shooting.

In a proper stance, your feet must be correctly positioned and your bridge arm should be comfortably extended on the table, with your hand preferably six to eight inches behind the cue ball. The forearm of the arm you stroke with should be perpendicular to the floor, making a perfect 90 degree angle. That holds no matter how low down you go on the cue. Your stoke arm must act like a pendulum, and the closer it is to perpendicular, the truer the arc of that pendulum will be. The whole idea is to make the platform that you shoot from as stable as possible.

Now, how far down over the cue should you go? The days of the nearly vertical shooter are long gone. Most players lean over to a point at which the torso is somewhere between horizontal and only about one third of the way to vertical. Aiming enters into it, but the degree of lean you adopt is a matter of physique and, to a certain extent, preference.

I'm relatively tall, but I'm also one of the players who goes to the

Ewa With Her Chin Down on Her Cue

max. When I shoot, my chin is lightly touching the shaft of the cue stick. I actually get a little callus under my chin when I've been playing a lot—and after just one game there's usually a faint streak under my chin from the chalk dust that is on every cue.

The reason I started to lean so low was a matter of comfort—and because it allowed me to aim the cue ball more accurately. I learned to play just as the popularity of straight pool was on the wane. Straight pool is more of a "position player's game" than a "shooter's game." Consequently, players tend to stand up higher because they need an overview of the layout of balls on the table.

Nowadays, the most popular games are nine ball (which is the game Paul Newman and Tom Cruise played in *The Color of Money*) and eight ball. In both, you are restricted in the balls at which you can aim. Easy shots are usually the exception rather than the rule. Consequently, the principle requirement is aiming—and, to me, the lower my head is, the easier it is to aim.

By choosing to lightly rest my chin on the cue, I inadvertently came up with a technique that adds to the consistency of my stance. I am already as low as it is possible to go. That might be a bit extreme for you, but if it is comfortable, try it.

The point is to learn what is the proper stance for you. Concentrate on how you position your feet, check if your weight is evenly distributed (a slight bias in favor of the rear foot is permissible), make sure your bridge arm is comfortably positioned six to eight inches behind the cue ball, keep your stroke arm perpendicular, and check to see that your chin is at the usual distance from the cue stick.

Then do it again. And again. And again. Practice it. Practice. Practice. Practice. Make it second nature.

Take the time to learn the fundamentals, practice the fundamentals, then forget the fundamentals—that's how integral they should be to your game. Pool is challenging enough without having to analyze your stance every time you get ready to shoot.

GRIP

There's a great deal of confusion over the proper way to hold a cue stick. Where? How tightly? In the fingers? Or in the palm?

Obviously the grip has to be someplace on the handle, or "wrap." The precise point depends greatly on your physique. Someone with very long arms probably won't feel comfortable gripping a cue stick in the same spot used by someone with very short arms. The first thing to do is to determine the balance point of the cue stick. Take the stick with one hand, hold out the index finger of your other hand, and place the cue on your index finger to determine where that particular stick is balanced. Usually the balance point will be in the far forward portion, although it might even be in front of the wrap.

Then pick up the cue stick about three to six inches behind the balance point. Simply pick it up with the hand you will use to make your stroke.

In all likelihood, the way you are holding the cue at this moment is probably the best all-around grip to begin with. The cue stick should be resting at a point slightly behind the tips of your fingers in a cradle formed by the aligned first joints of your fingers. Most of the pressure with which you are holding the cue stick is being exerted by the thumb and first three fingers. The pinky essentially rests behind the fingers and provides for guidance and balance.

I hold the cue mostly with my middle and ring fingers with very little pressure coming from my index finger.

Remember not to grip the cue stick too tightly. That's why I don't like a full-hand grip like you might use on a tennis racket. That type of grip, with the cue stick almost in the palm, results in a tendency to grip the cue too tightly in tough situations. If you suddenly put a death grip on the cue, you will throw your stroke mechanics off. Even at the best of times, too firm a grip will cause your wrist to tighten and you will lose the fluidity you need.

I think it was Lee Trevino who said that you should grip a golf club as if you were holding a live bird in your hand. That is a good analogy, but I prefer to think that your grip should be the one you would use to hold a one-year-old child by the hand. You must be gentle and tender, yet firm enough not to lose control if the child tries to take off.

BRIDGES

The hand with which you support the cue stick is called the bridge. As the name implies, its prime requirement is to be solid. The bridge you

Ewa's Grip

form is the platform that guides the cue. Until you are able to build the firmest possible bridge to support every shot, your game will remain erratic. If you shoot from the firmest possible bridge, it follows that your ability to control that white ball will be improved, and your accuracy at pocketing balls should be more consistent.

Let's review the basic bridges and how they are built.

OPEN BRIDGE. This is sometimes called the beginner's bridge. It is a very natural and comfortable position. The open bridge consists of little more than placing your hand on the table or rail, arching it slightly, and letting the fingers splay out just a bit to form a wider base. Your thumb should rest against your index finger. The cue stick rides in the channel formed between the thumb and the forefinger.

The Open Bridge

There are times when an open bridge will be necessary, and you should practice and feel confident in using it. But there is a far more reliable bridge that — despite its nickname — beginners should learn.

PROFESSIONAL BRIDGE. The professional bridge creates a more stable platform for the cue, however, its main benefit is that it helps the cue tip to stay on the cue ball for a longer time. It provides you with an extra degree of control. The problem is that, like the golf swing, it may feel unnatural at first and it has to be learned. We'll do it by the numbers:

Step 1. Place the heel of your bridge hand on the table between six and eight inches behind the cue ball. In playing conditions

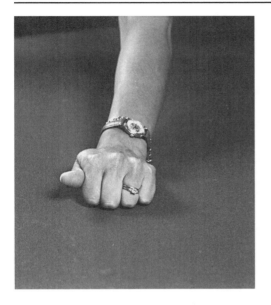

Making the Professional Bridge,
Step 1

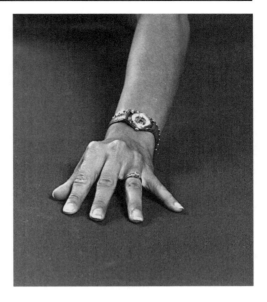

Making the Professional Bridge,
Step 2

the distance might have to vary depending on the type of shot you want to make, but try not to place your hand more than eight inches from the object ball. That is the point where most people begin to lose control and accuracy.

Step 2. Roll the tips of your pinky, ring, and middle fingers onto the table. The fingers should be splayed out as far as is tolerable in order to form the widest base (and therefore the most stable).

Step 3. Touch the pad of the thumb to the middle finger just about at the first joint. Let the forefinger buckle upwards. At first this might seem impossible, or at least uncomfortable. You'll quickly get used to it. Even if you feel like a contortionist at this moment you also can feel the rock-solid base you have formed.

Step 4. Rest the cue on your middle finger and curl your forefinger over the cue stick until it touches your thumb. With your thumb and your forefinger you have made a ring around the cue stick. At

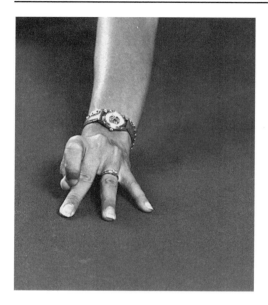

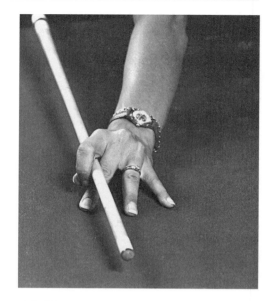

Making the Professional Bridge,
Step 3

Making the Professional Bridge,
Step 4

the same time you have formed a groove between your fore-finger and middle finger in which the cue stick will slide.

Remember, your bridge hand should not have any role in support-ing your body.

RAIL BRIDGE. This is actually a modification of the professional ("pro") bridge. It is used when the cue ball is sitting so close to a cushion that there is not room on the table to form the pro bridge. In the rail bridge, wrap the thumb under the hand and the forefinger around the cue.

FREESTANDING BRIDGE. You should be familiar with this bridge, but use it only when there is no choice—such as when your shot must be made over another ball on the table. The reason is simple: you are

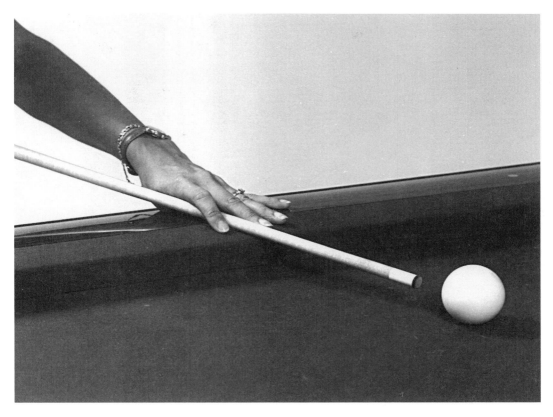

The Rail Bridge

forced to give away a lot of support. It is not as stable as any of the bridges previously mentioned.

The freestanding bridge requires that you lift the heel of your hand high enough to clear the interfering ball. And instead of trying to loop your index finger over the cue, the index finger should be used to provide support by being placed on the table, like the other three fingers. Place your thumb high up against the forefinger, forming a channel to guide the cue stick. It is much the same as a beginner bridge except that you are unable to rest the heel of your hand on the table. You should try to spread your fingers as far apart as possible in order to create the widest possible base.

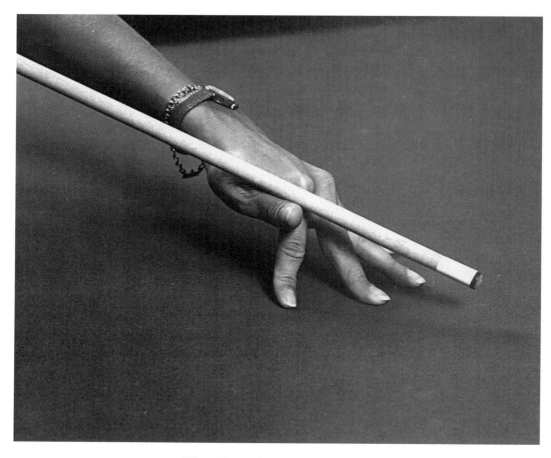

The Free Standing Bridge

MECHANICAL BRIDGE. Occasionally you will run into a shot you cannot reach. That's when the mechanical bridge comes into play. Use your bridge hand to keep the mechanical bridge steady and rested on the table.

There is a tendency to punch at the cue ball when using the mechanical bridge that must be overcome. You need to use a smooth follow-through here, just as in any other shot. Be careful you don't drop your elbow. It should be horizontal with the table for a straight follow-through.

The Mechanical Bridge

AIMING

Before we get into aiming, I'm going to ask you to imagine a scenario from another sport. Picture yourself as Joe Montana with time left for only one play in the Super Bowl. Your team is on the opponent's twelve-yard line and you need a touchdown to win. Obviously, you are going to throw a pass. Okay, Joe, you take the ball from the center, you drop back three steps, and you look . . . at the ball in your hand?

I don't think so.

You look downfield. You see an open receiver cutting across the end zone toward the goalpost and you throw the ball there, where you are looking. And, of course, being Joe Montana, you complete the pass and win the game.

Back to pool. What is the goal in this game? To sink the object ball. And in order to do that, you must hit the object ball with the cue ball. In other words, the cue ball is like the football. It is an intermediary. In each case, you must "hit" the receiver (or the object ball) just right in order to score. And in each case you must deliver the football, or the cue ball, with accuracy.

Now here comes the hard part. In neither case are you looking at the ball you control. Instead, you are keeping your eyes on the target when you throw the pass or make the pool stroke.

Being able to control the white ball is the foremost requirement of a good pool player (second, of course, to making the object ball). But that does not mean that you stare at the cue ball. The cue ball should become an extension of your arm and your hand; you should hit it correctly without having to look at it. The ball you must pay attention to as you're shooting is the object ball.

By the time you make your stroke, you should have made up your mind what you want to do—into which pocket you intend to sink the object ball, the precise spot where you will hit the cue ball, what English to put on it, what speed. You have visualized everything you need to know about the stroke. Now is the time to concentrate and aim the object ball into the pocket.

Your eyes might move between the cue ball and the object ball as you make your warm-ups, but when it is time to make the actual stroke, you must be looking at the object ball. Focus all your concentration there, and if you have made the right decisions and you have good stroke fundamentals, you will sink the ball.

Which again begs a question: Just where do you hit the object ball in order to sink it? The best way to accurately aim the object ball is to look at the center of the pocket into which you want to sink it and draw an imaginary line through the object ball. Where that imaginary line emerges from the object ball on the side opposite the pocket is the spot where you want the cue ball to hit the object ball (Diagram 3).

The idea of hitting the cue ball with the tip of a cue stick doesn't give people much trouble. They can just aim and shoot. But the idea of having to hit an object ball with another round object (the cue ball) sometimes often throws them for a loop. They seem to lose all sense of spatial relation, and they get all wound up trying to envision the angles.

Let's get the mystery out of it. The way you do that is to work back-

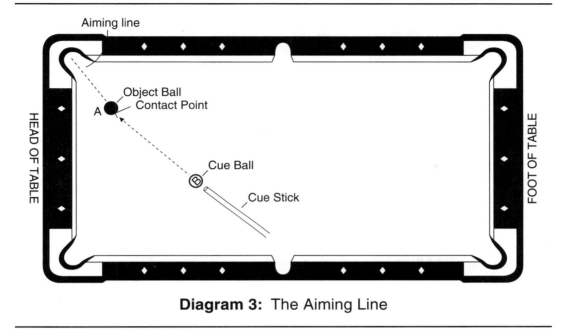

Diagram 3: The Aiming Line

ward. You start by finding the target spot on the object ball the same way we did it earlier — by drawing an imaginary line from the center of the pocket to the object ball. Then figure how the cue ball must be hit to make contact with that target. You do that in much the same manner — by drawing an imaginary line from the target spot on the object ball to the cue ball (Diagram 4).

Something that helps develop good aiming skills is to imagine a ball touching the object ball at the target spot. Call it a "ghost" ball if that helps you reinforce the concept. Imagine the cue ball taking the place of the "ghost" ball (Diagram 5). This type of visualization will quickly become second nature.

You can make it even more vivid in practice by actually placing a "ghost" ball at the spot where the cue ball should hit the object ball. Then, just before you take your stance, remove the "ghost" ball but keep visualizing it.

And remember to follow through and keep your head down after making your shot. I know it is tempting to bob up to see how you did, but that is a sure way to wreck your stroke mechanics. Even if you get

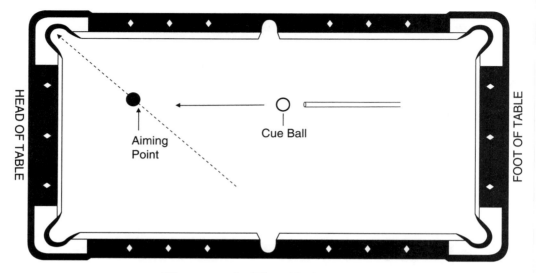

Diagram 4: The Aiming Point

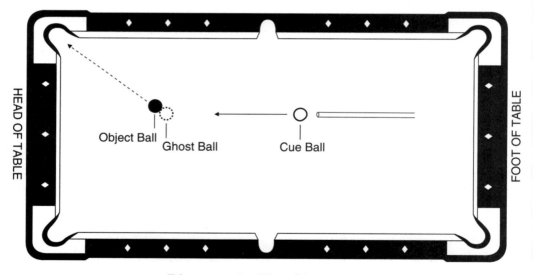

Diagram 5: The Ghost Ball

away with it a couple of times, eventually your game is going to come apart, and correcting the habit of looking up is not easy—ask any of your friends who play golf. Besides, how many times do you think Joe Montana got to see Dwight Clark or Jerry Rice haul in one of his touchdown passes? By that time he was usually flat on his back with a three hundred-pound lineman sprawled across his chest. Just keep your head down and think about how much luckier you are.

STROKE

Stroke is what eventually separates the "players" from the pros.

Let's go step-by-step through the stroke from start to follow-through. Well, not from absolute square one. Let's assume that you've decided on your shot, stepped up into your stance, have the cue stick gripped properly, made the bridge, aimed . . . and now what?

Once you go down into your shooting stance, the only thing that should move on the actual shot is your shooting arm. It should pivot at the elbow and swing smoothly and continuously through an arc that allows your wrist to pivot with the cue stick, sending it moving smoothly forward. The cue should maintain as level a plane as possible.

It sounds so easy. So does a golf shot. And there are some people who have great natural golf swings and some people who have great natural pool strokes. Just as there are any number of top-line players in both sports who have labored to develop a good stroke.

Stance is important, but the key to a good stroke is timing. Take a slow drawback, maybe a pause, and then thrust the cue stick through the cue ball. The point in the stroke at which the elbow and, subsequently, the wrist make the pivots is the secret.

Timing is the determinant.

There are clues as to when—and why—your stroke goes wrong. Even pros lose their stroke. Under ideal conditions you want to keep the cue stick as parallel as possible to the table. Watch where the tip of your cue ends up on your follow-through. If it is arcing sharply upward, it could be a sign of a problem. Many people jack up the back of the cue, but all that costs you is a possible loss of consistency and accuracy.

Plus there's a good chance that you are going to end up with unwanted spin on the cue ball.

The two most common stroke errors are dropping the shoulder or the head. It is quite common to see players maintain perfect form on their warm-ups, only to suddenly drop their shooting arm shoulder on the actual shot. That is a disaster. It's like a golfer who takes a perfect stance, makes an even takeback, then "puts something extra" into his swing ... and watches the ball sail into the rough. There is no rough on a pool table, but you're going to have a rough time if you get in the habit of dropping your shoulder.

Here are just a couple of things that go wrong when you drop your shoulder. Your elbow must also move in compensation, and when that happens, the pivot point for your lower arm is different than it was on your warm-ups. Not only is your stance thrown out of alignment, but—because the pivot point has moved—your timing will suffer and so will your aiming.

Lifting the head is another problem pool shares with golf. Players seem compelled to pull their heads up to watch their shots.

Both of these stroke errors can be diagnosed, and then cured, by maintaining a proper follow-through. Stay in position until the cue tip is four to five inches beyond where it struck the cue ball. At that point it should still be on the aiming line and almost parallel to the surface of the table. If it is not, you are probably guilty of one of these two errors.

Here is a table drill that will help you perfect your shot mechanics. Simply shoot several balls directly into a corner pocket from a spot at the other end of the table. Do not think of this as an aiming drill; you should concentrate on your follow-through. Draw the cue stick back slowly, shoot through the ball, and watch that follow-through.

If the tip of the cue goes off the aiming line, or if the cue tip pops upward, something is wrong with your stroke mechanics. In order, my checklist of things to examine is:

- stance
- dropping the shoulder
- lifting the head
- suddenly gripping the cue too tightly

Do this drill for soft, medium, and hard shots. Often errors will be confined to just one type of shot. Don't be disappointed by the drill's simplicity. It is an effective way to both perfect and diagnose your stroke.

SPEED

How much speed—or pace—you put on the cue ball is integral with your stroke mechanics. It is essential that you develop a "touch." If you hit the cue ball with the same amount of energy each time, you are obviously cutting your shot-making options, not realizing the full potential of English and just about giving up on playing position. Learn the effects of speed and it will open your eyes to all manner of possibilities.

There's no book, and no video, that is going to teach you this. The only way that knowledge comes about is through experience.

Set up the same shot over and over again and hit the cue ball with different pacing to gauge what happens. Do it with straight-in shots, then with moderate cut shots, and then with heavy cuts.

Generally, the harder the shot, the more difficult it will be to control. A power shot may make it look like you are shooting with confidence—and it may intimidate an opponent for that very reason—but your aim better be dead-on. Simply put, pockets "don't take the ball as well" when it comes in at warp speed.

Conversely, too soft a shot decreases the allowable margin of error on even a slightly mishit or misaimed shot. This fact comes as a revelation to many people. But after they hit the same shot repeatedly and discover that they have far less problem sinking the object ball with a moderately forceful shot, they adjust their natural pacing, usually with dramatic improvement in their game.

Often people "pull up short" with the cue stick when they take such soft shots. Follow-through is just as important in maintaining good stroke mechanics on these shots as it is on any other type of shot. Remember, the idea is to use speed to get around the table for position without having to use extreme English on your shots.

CENTER ENGLISH

If you want to consider yourself an even moderately competent pool player—of any game of pool—you must know where the cue ball will go after a shot. And that requires applying some spin to the cue ball.

With English you can make the cue ball trail the object ball. Or you can have it back up as if the object ball was just sprayed by a skunk. You can make the cue ball curve to the left or curve to the right or stop dead in its tracks. And you can make the other balls on the table dance as well.

I realize that some of this must sound like those late-night infomercials. But instead of fanciful testimony about the benefits of real estate investment or meditative chanting, you can be assured that "English" is nothing more than the principles of physics applied to a cue ball.

Specifically: for every action, there is an equal and opposite reaction. Keep that in mind and English becomes comprehensible and predictable.

CENTER ENGLISH — STOP SHOT.   This shot causes the cue ball to stop dead in its tracks when it hits the object ball. What happens is that essentially 100 percent of the cue ball's momentum is transferred to the object ball. Strike the cue ball at its centerpoint, or just below center (Diagrams 6, 7). You must execute this shot with authority because what you must do is push the cue ball across the table instead of allowing it to roll. The farther the object ball is from the cue ball, the firmer (and/or lower) you must hit on the cue ball. The cue ball might start to rotate a bit, but the goal is to keep it from turning over too much and

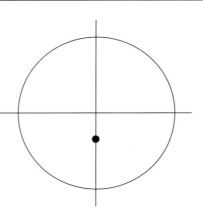

Diagram 6: The Stop Shot — Aiming Point on the Cue Ball

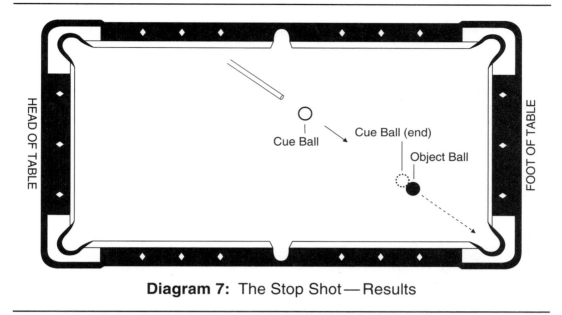

Diagram 7: The Stop Shot — Results

developing its own inertia. (Use a striped ball instead of the cue ball in order to be better able to observe and understand the dynamics.)

The stop shot works best when there is very little or no angle required to make the shot — that is, a straight-in.

You can use an angle to your advantage, however. A sharp center hit on the cue ball will allow you to "punch" the cue ball to the left or right in order to gain position.

HIGH ENGLISH — FOLLOW SHOT. Simply aim at the upper portion of the cue ball and follow through with a smooth stroke. This capitalizes on the natural tendency of a ball to roll in a forward direction (Diagrams 8, 9).

With practice, you will learn the proper amount of force to use in order to gain position with the cue ball for your next shot.

While small degrees of follow are fairly easy to gauge, extreme follow is not as simple as it might appear. Watch a pro hit a ball with high English and you may see the cue ball almost stop for a microsecond when it contacts the object ball (if there is little angle). Then spin takes

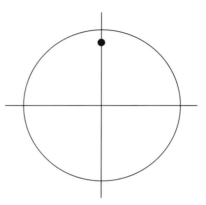

Diagram 8: The Follow Shot—Aiming Point on the Cue Ball

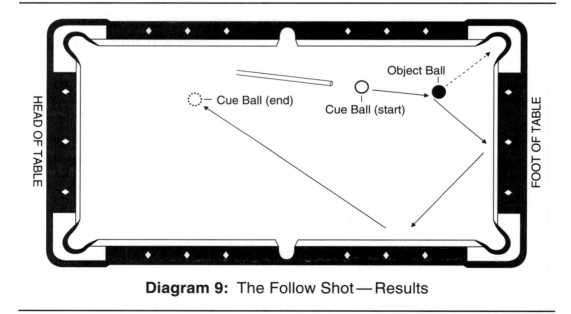

Diagram 9: The Follow Shot—Results

over and the cue ball resumes its path, seemingly rejuvenated and with new momentum.

Interestingly, a very softly made long shot will turn into a "follow" shot even if you hit quite low on the cue ball. Remember, the cue ball's natural tendency is to spin in the direction it is traveling. With a soft shot, that natural tendency often is enough to overcome the energy of the low English you might have applied.

LOW ENGLISH — DRAW.   When you hit with low English, even though the cue ball is going forward, it has backward spin on it (Diagram 10). Instead of rolling the natural way, it's rotating just the opposite . . . and it will behave in a similarly unnatural manner upon contact with the object ball. It will back up instead of following the object ball. Again, speed and the amount of English applied determine how much the cue ball will "draw," as this backup motion is called.

This is one of the more difficult shots to master. It puts a premium on good stroke mechanics. Proper follow-through is absolutely crucial.

Here is a practice drill to help understand and master draw:

• Set up the cue ball and an object ball along an imaginary line between the side pockets (Diagram 11).

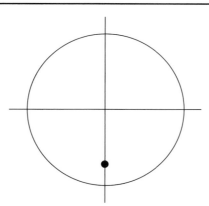

Diagram 10: The Draw Shot—Aiming Point on the Cue Ball

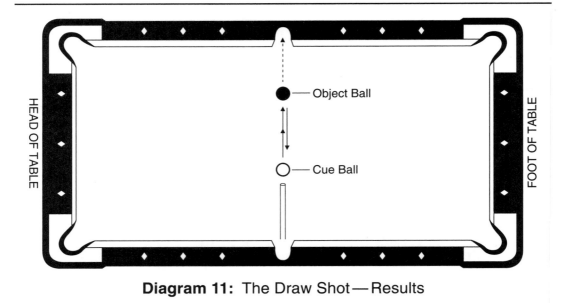

Diagram 11: The Draw Shot — Results

- Shoot straight through the cue ball with low English. (Make sure you keep your wrist nice and loose and follow through to the maximum — do not "pound" the ball or try to send it off at a hundred miles per hour. Put the emphasis on the smoothness, not the power.)

- *Watch as the cue ball comes rolling back toward you.*

After you feel comfortable and confident doing this, try to draw the cue ball back far enough to scratch into the side pocket on your side of the table, making sure, of course, that you continue to sink the object ball on each shot.

When you can scratch the cue ball on a regular basis into the side pocket nearest you, little by little increase the distance between the cue ball and the object ball as you continue to try this shot. Remember, the farther away the object ball is, the more stoke and power will be required to scratch.

This drill is a worthwhile one for experts as well as beginners to determine speed and control.

You must keep your grip firm but loose on a draw shot. Remember, grip the cue stick as if you are holding the hand of a toddler.

SIDE SPIN

Until now, all of our discussion has involved hitting somewhere along the centerline of the cue ball, either high (follow) or low (draw).

Now we are going to strike the cue ball at a point that is off the centerline. Hitting the cue ball to the left or right of center radically affects the outcome of any shot. It changes the path of the cue ball/ after contact—from an infinitesimal amount to putting a wild hook into the route—and it can allow you to leave the cue ball almost anywhere you want on the table.

Played correctly, side spin can bring your game to new levels. Played incorrectly or played without full understanding—as is more often the case—the results can be disastrous.

Yet, maybe because it is so dramatic, side spin is what most beginners want to learn right after they master the pro bridge. The hazard is that if you start shooting with side spin before you are a competent player, you're just going to confuse yourself. Big–time. My rule of thumb is that until a student has gotten to the point where he is comfortable running fifteen open balls two or three times with just center English, I will not even let him think about side spin.

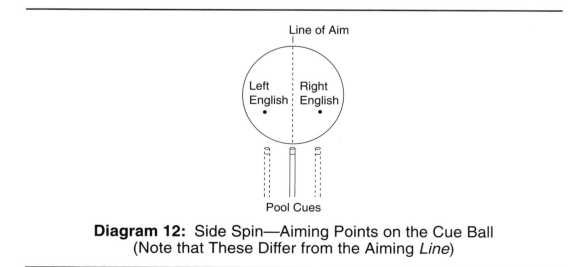

Diagram 12: Side Spin—Aiming Points on the Cue Ball
(Note that These Differ from the Aiming *Line*)

Even then, I regard this type of shot as a necessary evil because whenever you put spin on the ball—particularly side spin—you're making the basic shot that much more difficult. Note that I said a "necessary" evil. You must understand these shots if you are going to master the tactical side of the game. Side spin is crucial in playing position pool.

The key to side spin is knowledge. You have to learn what will happen when you impart a particular type of spin. Start out with an easy shot. Place the object ball about eight to ten inches from a corner pocket and the cue ball about a foot farther away. Now sink the object ball, being careful to note the paths of both the object ball and the cue ball. Playing this shot with center English will cause the cue ball to come off the rail at angle B (Diagram 13), the "natural" angle.

Applying side spin will alter that angle. And it will alter it to varying degrees depending on how much side spin you apply. Left spin will cause the cue ball to come off short, or on a more acute angle, angle A (Diagram 14). Right spin will bring the cue ball off the rail at a wider angle, angle C (Diagram 15).

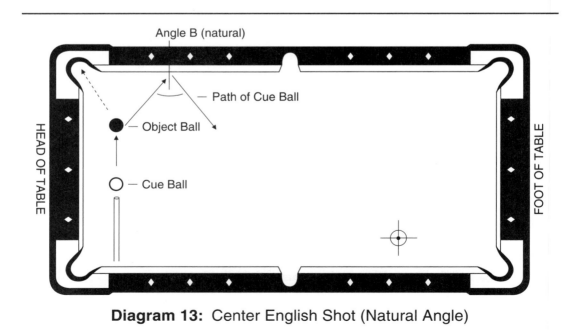

Diagram 13: Center English Shot (Natural Angle)

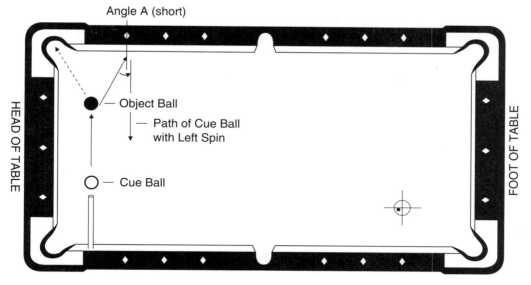

Diagram 14: Left English Shot (Short Angle)

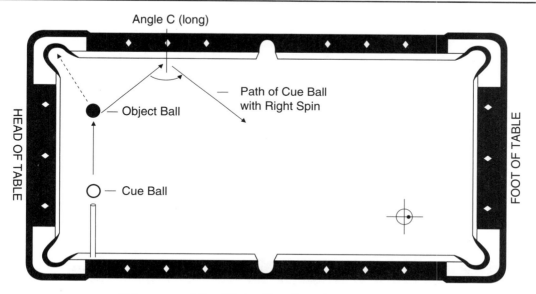

Diagram 15: Right English (Long Angle)

Don't overdo it. Hitting the cue ball a half to a full tip's width off the centerline will be sufficient to provide you with proof positive of how side spin changes the path of the ball.

Now that you are convinced, and have some experience with side spin, I have to tell you that there is no shortcut to learning how to gauge all these varying angles and vectors. Some people seem to have a better innate sense of what will happen when different amounts of side spin are used, but *everyone* must learn side spin through practice and experience.

Understanding side spin is the first step, but executing it properly can be a whole different matter. Most of the time it is difficult to see, but sometimes the cue ball actually curves a bit on shots hit with side spin. So if things are not difficult enough already, that means you also have to adjust your aiming point on the cue ball.

Here is a hint to help you line up a side spin shot. Aim as you normally would with regular (center) English, then move the cue over slightly in the direction that will allow you to apply the side spin you want, *making sure to keep parallel to the original line of aim.* Finally, make your stroke as you normally would.

Keeping the aiming point parallel to the perpendicular is absolutely crucial.

Obviously, if there are errors in your stroke mechanics—say, you are lifting the tip slightly at the instant of impact—these will be magnified on side English shots.

When learning side spin, you should start by practicing short shots and work your way up. As you will soon see, this is because the longer the shot, the more the cue ball will curve.

Want more? Now vary the speed with which you hit the cue ball. When you hit it slowly, the English is more pronounced. Probably that's the exact opposite of what you anticipated. It is a result of the cue ball's having more time to "grab" on the cloth and the rail. Hit the cue ball faster and it slides across the cloth, and the English is proportionally less.

If ever there was a case for practice, this is it. You have to know how to shoot with side spin to become a complete player, and that knowledge can only come through practice.

Above all, remember that it is a learnable technique. The difference between students is how long the learning process takes. For a lucky few, it comes easily and quickly. Others are not that lucky ... but keep in mind, it is a learnable technique.

I will repeat: keep those shots with a lot of side spin to a minimum. Center spin is generally the preferred shot because it allows you to have better control of the cue ball and it generally makes it easier to pocket the ball.

BANK SHOTS

You will not see bank shots—shots off a cushion—being taken very often when professionals are playing. That should tell you something.

Given the option between a bank shot and a cut shot, the pros will take the cut shot almost every time. Why? It is because you have more control on a cut than you do on a bank. The slightest variation in how a cushion plays can cause your bank shot to go astray. And these variations can range from actual dead spots in the cushion to the many results of heat and humidity (see the discussion of cushions in Chapter Two under "Tables") to just being slightly off in your aim.

But there are times when a bank shot is called for, so you had better know the fundamentals of how to make one. They begin—and pretty much end—with learning where to aim. I'm not going to go into any system of "playing the diamonds" here. Although it cannot hurt to learn various banking/kicking systems, I prefer to treat the bank shot like any other shot.

The way you learn the "whys" of bank shots is to shoot. In this case, shoot at the same spot on a cushion to see what the cue ball does. From one side of the table, shoot at the diamond closest to the side pocket on the opposite side (Diagram 16).

Shoot the cue ball with your normal, most comfortable, pacing. Then shoot it hard. Shoot soft. With top spin. Draw. Natural and reverse English. In each instance, observe the path of the cue ball off the cushion. Does it go long (come off the cushion at a wider angle than normal), or does it come off short (at a more acute angle)?

Now line up a series of object balls on your side of the table. Start shooting them into the same spot using the cue ball. Run the whole

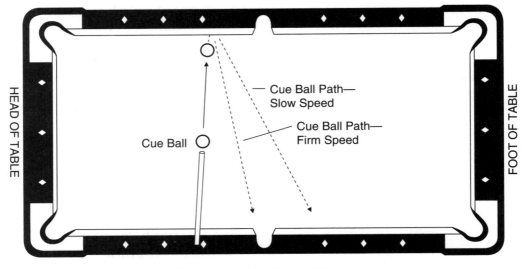

Diagram 16: Bank Shots

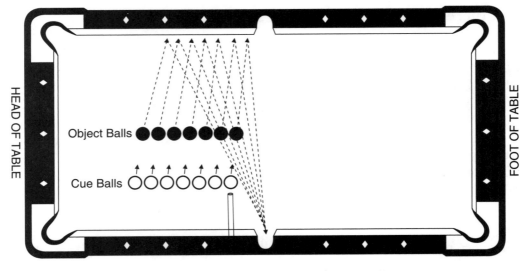

Diagram 17: The Bank Shot Drill

lineup using no English. Then repeat the sequence with various types of English and speed as you did in the first drill. This time, make a note of how the object ball behaves.

From these drills you will learn when the balls will go long or short. You also will probably be convinced as to why most of the pros avoid bank shots given any reasonable option.

COMBINATION SHOTS

Combinations have always had a place in straight pool and eight ball, but with the growing popularity of nine ball it's even more important to have combos in your shot-making arsenal. In plainest terms, a combination is a shot in which the cue ball must hit an intervening ball (or *balls* in some circumstances), which will, in turn, strike the object ball.

The easiest way I can explain the process is to guide you through the required steps. First, stand at the pocket into which you expect to

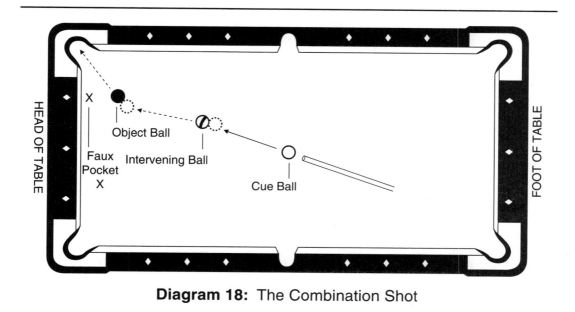

Diagram 18: The Combination Shot

sink the object ball. Look straight from the pocket to the object ball and trace an imaginary line from the pocket through the object ball (in much the same manner you now employ in basic aiming). That will determine the spot where the object ball must be struck, which again is like basic aiming (Diagram 18).

Here is where the aiming techniques diverge. Draw an imaginary line from that point on the object ball to the intervening ball (the one the cue ball will hit). That will give you the spot on the intervening ball at which you will aim the cue ball. Forget for the time being that the object ball even exists. The target of your aim is a point on the intervening ball that will "pocket" the intervening ball into faux pocket *X*.

Take your shot as if the intervening ball were the object ball. Do all your aiming and visualization without even worrying about the object ball. The *X* has become the faux pocket.

Concentrate on making a shot that hits that faux pocket perfectly. That means the ball you will be looking at as you shoot will actually be the intervening ball. (The only adjustment you should consider making is how hard you hit the intervening object ball, as it, in turn, must hit the *real* object ball with enough transferrable force to sink it.)

Combinations are low-percentage shots that often are best justified when, if you miss, you will leave the cue ball in a difficult spot for your opponent.

KISS SHOT. This is the "kiss" or "carom" shot. Essentially it is a combination, but instead of striking the object ball with the intervening ball, you will use the cue ball (Diagram 19). This requires a thorough knowledge of what the cue ball will do after it hits the first ball. Aim, pacing, and English all can be factors in determining the path the cue ball will take.

Everyone has a favorite type of "show" shot, and I must confess that the kiss shot is mine. I like to practice it by playing what I call "kiss pool" (or scratch pool). It consists of throwing, for example, nine balls out on the table, then playing each object ball by striking it *first* off the cue ball, pocketing the object ball. If anything is going to give you a feel for the path one ball will take after hitting another ball, this drill is it. It's amazing the sense of confidence it creates. Plus you have the satisfaction of hearing those balls go into the pockets. I highly recommend kiss pool, not only as a teaching aid, but to keep practice sessions from getting repetitive.

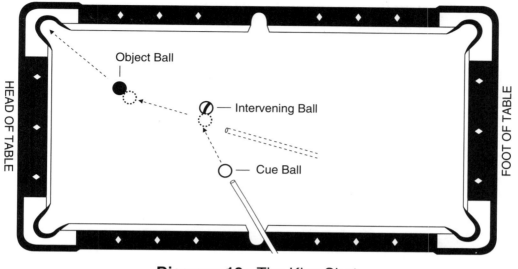

Diagram 19: The Kiss Shot

THROW SHOTS. The shot in Diagram 20 may look impossible, since the shot is lined up for the cushion and the balls are touching, which means you cannot cut the object ball into the pocket. Here is where the throw shot comes in. If shot from the left side, the ball will throw into the side pocket. This shot can also be controlled and altered with speed and English. It is very useful playing straight pool, but will also come up in the other games, so make sure it is a shot you work on (Diagram 20).

SPECIALTY SHOTS

In addition to bank and combination shots, other shots might be called for under specific conditions. Some of them, as you will see, have a "high-risk factor," quite literally.

JUMP SHOT. This shot, too, has become more prevalent with the growing popularity of nine ball, since there is always a designated ball you *must* hit. When all, or a portion, of a ball on the table blocks the path the cue ball must travel to hit the object ball, the jump shot may be your only reasonable means of making a legal hit.

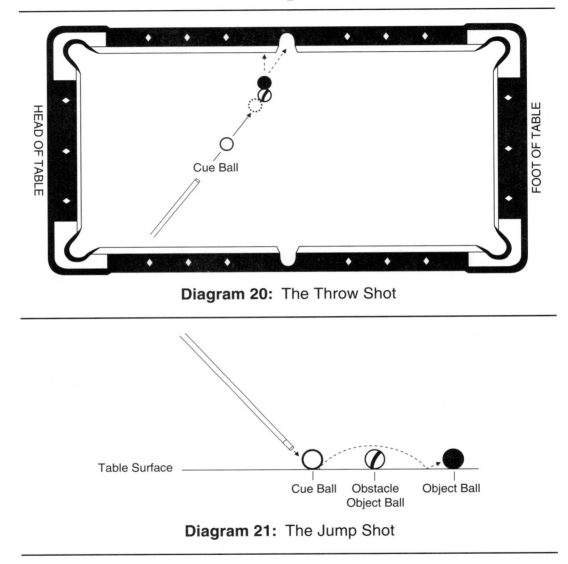

Diagram 20: The Throw Shot

Diagram 21: The Jump Shot

Aim the shot just as you would normally, avoiding any side English. Then elevate the back of your cue stick to a radical angle, and shoot down on the cue ball with a firm stroke (Diagram 21). The angle you use depends on how far you need to jump. The cue ball will actually hop over the intervening ball. This is *not* an easy shot, but it will come in handy from time to time, so practice it.

Shoot with a firm stroke. If you need extra elevation on the jump, a "jump cue" might be of help. These cue sticks are short and weighted differently to help you feel comfortable with this high-angle type of shooting, and they will allow you to jump a shot more consistently and with more arc.

If you play nine ball with any regularity, you need this shot in your repertoire. Practice this, but at a friend's house on his or her table because this shot actually leaves a small nick in the cloth.

CURVE SHOT.   In some situations it's to your advantage to play a curve shot instead of a jump shot. For example, when the object ball is close to a cushion and there is a strong chance that the cue ball will continue to jump—right off the table. In this case, a much safer option is the curve—or the half-massé—shot.

Aiming to miss the obstacle ball, elevate the back of the cue and hit down on the cue ball, adding side English (to the right to make the cue ball curve right, to the left to make the cue ball curve left). The extreme English will cause the cue ball to curve around any intervening ball(s), and then straighten out to make the hit (Diagrams 22, 23). The amount of English and the pace at which you shoot the cue ball determine the amount of curve that is imparted.

It goes without saying that you must practice this shot to get a feel for hitting a curve ball. And remember, as with all strong English shots, the softer you hit the more the English will grab.

MASSÉ SHOT.   This might be the most difficult shot of all. It also carries a risk of miscueing—a fact that turns poolroom owners prematurely gray when they see it being attempted. The massé should be attempted only when desperate measures are called for. It is similar to the curve, but in this case you shoot down on the cue ball in a virtually perpendicular manner. The cue stick is at a correct angle for a normal shot, vertical instead of horizontal (Diagrams 24, 25). It's not a good percentage shot, although there are some pros who are absolute masters of the massé.

When executed properly, the massé causes the cue ball to hook violently. When executed improperly, the table felt is at risk. You should practice this shot—but on a neighbor's table.

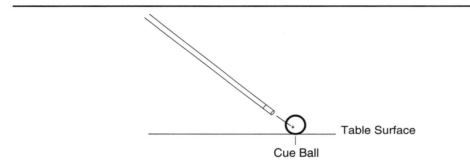

Diagram 22: The Curve Shot—Aiming Point on the Cue Ball

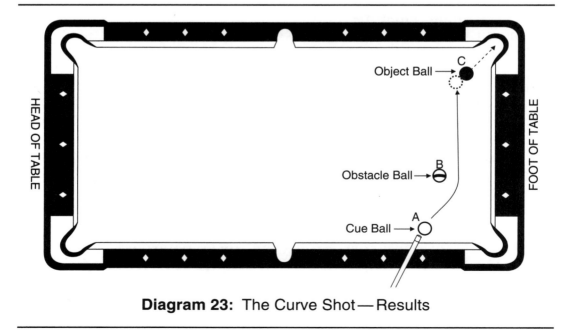

Diagram 23: The Curve Shot—Results

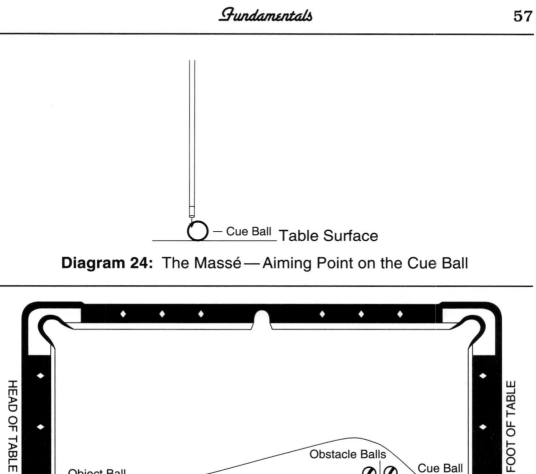

Diagram 24: The Massé — Aiming Point on the Cue Ball

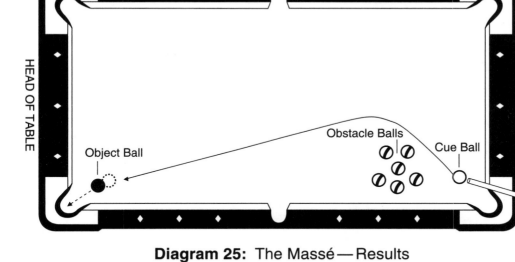

Diagram 25: The Massé — Results

4

Mental Fundamentals

*W*hen I first moved to the United States and started to play pool here, something unique and unsettling occurred. I simply could not play well in tournaments.

What made it so unsettling was that I could not find any reason for the falloff. I had been taught how to analyze my game, how to break it down into the fundamentals so as to pinpoint any problem. So I reviewed everything about my game: stance, grip, stroke, everything. Sure, I found that I was making a couple of little errors, but nothing big.

In fact, I was pleased with the way I played in practice. But still, when it came to tournaments, I couldn't shake the feeling that it wasn't me out there.

That should have been my first clue. It wasn't me out there.

In Europe, I knew my opponents. I felt comfortable traveling to countries where the language, the food, even the times at which meals were eaten was somewhat familiar. I was still only a teenager, but I was ready to play against anyone. Looking back on it, maybe my success was helped by the fact that I *was* a teenager. There's a lot to be said for that "youthful invulnerability" we hear so much about.

The secret was confidence.

The United States was unfamiliar territory. Europe was diverse, but I grew up in the midst of that diversity and I was not surprised by it. But the United States?

From the players to the customs to the pace of life, it was all very new to me. And I know now that my confidence level dropped. The mechanics of my game were still good. My stroke had not suddenly deteriorated. But I had made myself vulnerable because the way I thought about the game—or didn't think about it—had changed. I also felt I had a lot to prove, putting unnecessary pressure on myself.

It took me a while to pull it all back. I learned not only how important confidence is to your game, but how to maintain that confidence.

The first, and most important, thing to realize is that you can't just tell yourself "Be confident" and think that's all it will take. Just as with the other fundamentals we have discussed—the physical fundamentals that underlie your game—you need to learn the basic mental fundamentals so well that they become second nature. Then you can concentrate on the game that's on the table at that moment.

And the more you concentrate on the game at hand, the better your mind-set becomes. It's a closed loop that is always expanding and causing you to play better: the more confident you are in your game, the more you can concentrate on the game; therefore, the better your game becomes; which, in turn, builds still more confidence.

Okay, but that leaves us one big question. How do you get this loop of confidence started?

I found out when my own loop of confidence broke when I began to live in the United States. Well, *broke* is probably too strong a word. Let's just say it was pushed out of shape. Badly.

The secret is staying in the game every second. Pool is one of the few sports that turns over the game to just one player at a time. As a result, it almost encourages your mind to wander. And if you have a lot of other concerns that have nothing to do with the game at hand—and who doesn't?—that's exactly what can happen. Your mind will take you out of the game.

You hear athletes from tight ends to tennis players talking about it. Focus. It's gotten to the point where it is almost a sports cliché. But that's just the point. If many successful athletes cite "focus" as their secret, or as the reason why their team suddenly seemed to come to life, you can figure that there's something to it.

But the human body doesn't come equipped with an automatic focus button. It isn't like a 35-mm camera. So you have to practice focusing just like any other fundamental. And the more you practice it, the more natural it will become.

If you are going to be serious about pool, play—and practice—seriously. Set a rhythm, a pace, to your practice sessions. But pool should not be like an aerobics session, where you simply do the same exercises over and over again to a heavy tempo set by Salt-n-Pepa.

To put a slight twist on a line from a popular advertising campaign: Don't just do it, but think about it.

It is important to keep in the back of your mind that every shot you take is an opportunity to learn something new: about yourself, about stroke mechanics, about how a table plays. It might not be an earth-shaking discovery, but every time you play you should come away with a bit more insight into the game of pool.

Which means you have to stay in the game even when your opponent has the table. Think. Think as if you are going to be taking the next shot on every shot. Create a rhythm and a pattern to your play. For example: If you feel most comfortable taking three warm-up strokes, take those three warm-ups every time. If you need four warm-ups for a sharp-angle cut shot or a long shot, by all means, take four warm-ups.

Whatever the rhythm, just make sure that you always perform some little ritual that sets the right rhythm for *you*. Don't allow yourself to be rushed, or become hesitant. It is the familiarity that counts. You've made this shot before! Here's that same rhythm again. One ... two ... three, shoot. You can't help but be more confident when you are on familiar ground.

It is easier to keep focused in game situations. But there are times, even then, when you lose it, and generally at the worst of times. I discovered this when I arrived in the United States and became distracted by the constant newness of my surroundings. When my opponents had the table, I can recall my eyes flickering around, checking out play on other tables, scoreboards, how people were dressed, almost everything except what I should have been concentrating on—what was happening on the table where I was playing.

Thus, when I got the table, I always felt as if I were scrambling to find the best shot. I was confused and I had lost my rhythm.

Finally, I remembered something that I had been taught by the late Swedish pool champion Bjorn Johnson: If you come up to the table and are bewildered as to what your next shot should be, that is a dead giveaway you were not concentrating. You should approach the table, every time, with a shot in mind. You might change that choice when you further analyze the possibilities—that's all right. But if you pick up your cue without a clue, you have lost focus.

That was it.

You have to go into what I call a "concentration coma." It's not that difficult. The basic rule is that even when you are sitting, you should continue to be shooting that rack. Stay on the table in your own mind.

When you feel that concentration coma slipping away, get back on that table. Think through every shot.

There are devices that may help reinforce your concentration coma. Instead of constantly reviewing table layouts, study your opponents, their expressions, how they move about the table. See how zeroed-in they are.

Nowadays, I often study my opponents even before the game begins. By seeing how intently they are playing, I can sort of draw from them. It's almost as if their intensity is catching.

Be careful, however, because the reverse is also true. If people around you have lost their focus, you have to be doubly vigilant to maintain yours.

This is particularly true in poolrooms where the social aspect can sometimes outweigh the competition. By all means be social, but don't get in the habit of thinking up witty rejoinders when you should be deciding whether to go for the side pocket or take a safety.

Even at home, don't have the television on when you are practicing. You are shortchanging yourself and your game if you think you increase your pleasure by half watching MTV while half practicing kiss shots.

Practice is a "no-risk" time to expand that loop of confidence. Too many people spend most of their time practicing what they are already good at. I'll admit, it is great fun to hear those balls tumbling into a pocket, but in the long run you'll get more out of practice by working on your weaknesses.

To avoid frustration while practicing difficult shots, make sure you set a system of rewards. If, for instance, you have a natural touch for cut shots to a corner pocket, but have difficulty cutting into the side pocket, allow yourself one confidence-building corner cut for every three side pocket shots you take.

Once you start building that loop of confidence you'll find it builds upon itself. And even when your game goes off, you have a format in which you know you can restore it. You're dealing with someone who has been there.

Fortunately, even when I was having trouble getting past the first round in tournaments, I never lost my love of pool. That experience taught me that the only way to get the most out of the sport is to build and maintain a strong foundation in the fundamentals—both physical and mental.

5

Pattern Play — An Introduction

*A*t the heart of playing good pool and getting the maximum satisfaction out of the sport is identifying the patterns that will let you make the most of your abilities. You can have the greatest stroke and the surest aim, but if you are blind to the patterns you are not a complete pool player and you will constantly find yourself in more difficult situations than necessary. Not only that, but you will find yourself losing to players of less ability ... not every game, but far more than you should.

Anyone can improve his game by creating the mind-set that seeks patterns every time he looks at the table. You must think ahead, analyze what the table layout offers, weigh your particular strengths and weaknesses, and plot the strategy that will maximize both. On the next shot. The shot after that. And right up to the end of the game.

Form the ideal pattern in your mind. But always be willing to change that pattern when conditions dictate. That's what I mean when I say you should be constantly looking for patterns. It's part of the loop of confidence (see the previous chapter). But if you take a look at the table and irrevocably lock in on a pattern, a sequence that you are determined to stick to come what may, you would do better to forget all about patterns. I'm quite serious.

The idea is to stay flexible. To make the most out of what is offered. Many times a glance hit, a rebound off a cushion, a slight mishit or miscalculation will completely upset a pattern ... or present the opportunity for a better pattern. Always, always, always, be looking for a new pattern. Remember, the idea is to make things as easy on yourself as you can.

That said, let's take a look at the basic pattern thinking you should have for each of the major types of pool. Note that I said pattern thinking. I will show you how to think, not just how to play a particular shot.

6

Nine Ball

*T*he popularity of nine ball is exploding. In my opinion it is the most exciting of the major pool games. The tension is always there.

Nine ball is fast—it can take just seconds if the nine is pocketed on the break. And it is difficult—the fact that you must play the balls in numerical succession means that hard shots must be taken much more frequently than in eight ball or straight pool. And it is strategic, with safeties being a major factor in the game, not an admission that you don't think you can make any shots.

BREAKS

When I first came to the United States many of the players viewed the nine ball break as simply a way to get the balls into play and possibly pocket something. Now the requirement is to make an explosive break, making a ball and literally play position on the one ball with the cue ball.

The key is to hit the one full in the face (head-on). You can position the cue ball wherever you feel most comfortable in order to hit with your hardest stroke. But no matter at what angle it comes into the one, it must make a full flush hit. That aiming point is far more important than the power with which the cue ball hits—although from what you see in poolrooms, and even from some pros, you might get the impression that the opposite is true.

I am not saying that power is not important, it's just that aim is even more important. Watch the cue ball after the hit. If it takes off to one side or another, you're hitting off-center. If it comes back at you, it was struck with too-low English.

There are adjustments you can make to improve your power on the break, in order to improve your chances of pocketing a ball, that will not destroy your normal stroke mechanics. Stand straighter than you would in your normal stance, which will allow you to transfer your center of gravity straight forward as you shoot. A power break is still a pool stroke, not a two-wood shot.

Even if you normally play with your bridge arm fully extended, cock it slightly so that you will be able to follow through freely with your entire body.

It's up to each individual as to what bridge to use. Personally, I prefer the open bridge for a nine ball break, but the closed (professional) bridge is more common.

PATTERNS

Let's say the balls have been broken and I have the table. Immediately, I look at the table and make a very fast rough plan. In seconds I see the layout and figure that the one is going to go over here. I'll make the two in this pocket, the three over here, the four, the five. Pretty much the whole table. Very rarely will it pan out exactly that way, but you have to have an overall concept in mind.

Now it's time to get down to a hard analysis. I usually begin with the third ball I plan to sink. Is the three open? Can it be pocketed? Where would I want the cue ball to be to most easily make the shot? If I had the cue ball in my hand and could put it down anywhere on the table to make that shot, where would that be?

Then I go backward in my thinking, to the two ball. How can I most easily get the cue ball to that spot after sinking the two? Where should the cue ball be so that I don't have to make it travel more than necessary?

Then I back up and go through the same procedure with the one in relationship to the two. I form the pattern by working backward.

So when I shoot the one, I also have the three in mind. Because of this, many times you'll find that the table layout is such that you will be better off playing the "wrong" shot in order to deal with a problem that is coming up.

Say there is a cluster of balls that will have to be broken up: can you break them by taking a side pocket cut instead of a straight corner shot? Or you see that the four and the five are frozen. So you plan from the outset to play a safety off the three.

The problems and variations are endless. The point is that you should always picture what you intend to do well beyond the shot you will take next. As long as you have a pattern in mind—even at the novice level— you have the advantage over a player who just gets up there and shoots the balls in. Even if that player is a better shot maker.

A few words about safeties. Nine ball is a game in which dramatic shots occur frequently. Maybe that's the reason why some people develop a sort of negative attitude about playing safeties. They'll go for the pocket every time. That aggressiveness is admirable in middle linebackers, but it does not make for consistently winning nine ball. Safeties must play an integral part in your planning. They are not a concession; they are part of winning game strategy.

Safeties allow you to gain an advantage in several ways. They present your opponent with a difficult situation that you have devised—anything from a long shot to a "snooker," where your opponent's object ball is blocked by another ball. You also have a greater potential for having a good shot when your opponent misses. And you will gain a "ball in hand" if your opponent cannot make contact with the lowest number ball on the table. There are huge benefits from playing safeties. Don't be hesitant about making the most of them.

Thus, the basic technique for formulating a game plan for nine ball is the following:

- Make a flash analysis of the table.

- In most cases, concentrate on the third ball you will be shooting and fine-tune your plan backward from that point.

- Don't hesitate to include safeties in your strategy.

- Be alert, and ready to change your pattern.

- Don't lose focus when there are only a couple of balls left on the table. When all of the big problems appear to have been solved, a lot of people "let down," and you see them missing position and blowing easy outs on the last two or three balls.

- Don't miss the nine!

PATTERNS EXAMPLE #1. Here is an open table with five balls left (see Diagrams 26 to 29). It is important to play position to stay on the correct side of the object ball in order to make it as easy on yourself as possible to get position on the following balls. The crucial play here is to come out on the correct side of the eight for easy position on the nine.

A. Play the five ball to drift up for position on the six using center English (Diagram 26).

B. With high center English, bring the cue ball off the rail for slight angle position on the seven (Diagram 27).

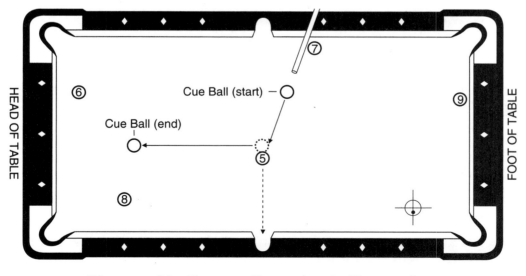

Diagram 26: Patterns Example #1: Shot on the 5

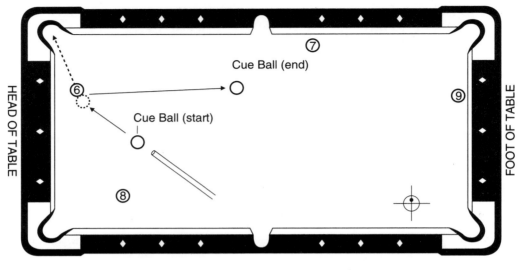

Diagram 27: Patterns Example #1: Shot on the 6

C. With low left English, draw the cue ball off the seven and come out on the correct side of the eight (Diagram 28).

D. Now you have a perfect shot to land for an easy tap-in on the nine. Just hit the cue ball with some right-hand English to make sure to avoid the scratch in the lower right-hand corner (Diagram 29).

PATTERNS EXAMPLE #2. Again, the eight is the key. Being on the "correct" side of that ball is vital for a clear straight shot on the nine (see Diagrams 30 to 33).

A. Play the five with high left English to bring the cue ball slightly to the right of the six (Diagram 30).

B. Draw off the six with low left English to come out properly off the rail, leaving an angle on the seven (Diagram 31).

C. Pocket the seven with low left English, drawing the cue ball back for the eight (Diagram 32).

D. Just hit the eight with low right English to float up for a straight-in corner pocket shot on the nine (Diagram 33).

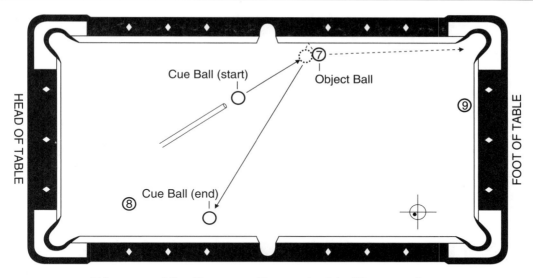

Diagram 28: Patterns Example #1: Shot on the 7

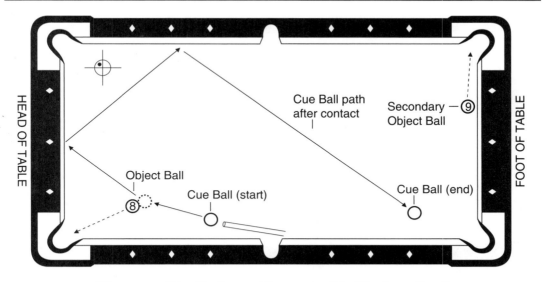

Diagram 29: Patterns Example #1: Shot on the 8

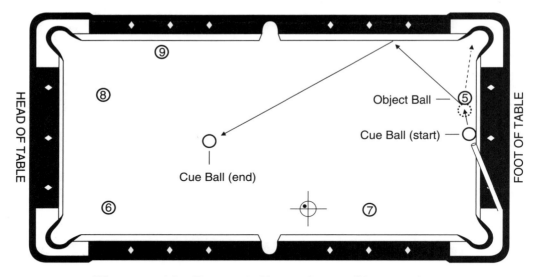

Diagram 30: Patterns Example #2: Shot on the 5

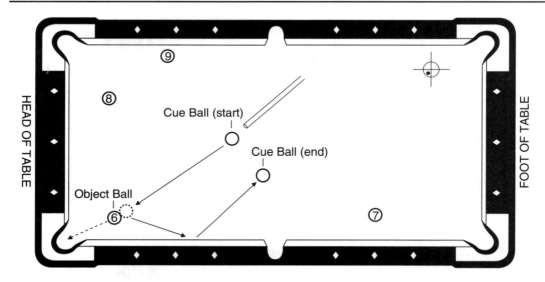

Diagram 31: Patterns Example #2: Shot on the 6

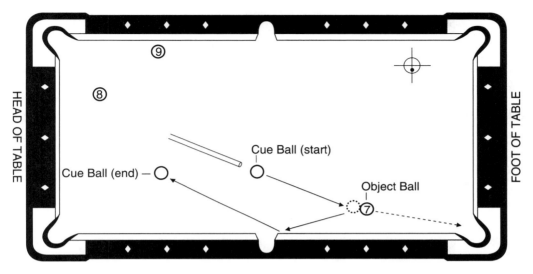

Diagram 32: Patterns Example #2: Shot on the 7

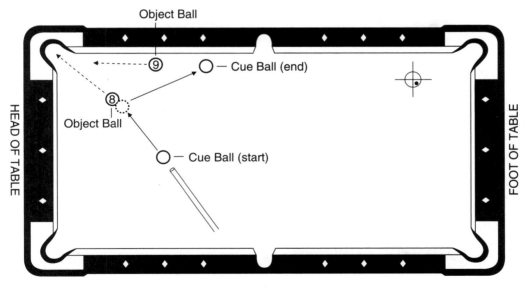

Diagram 33: Patterns Example #2: Shot on the 8

SAFETIES

SITUATION #1.   Shoot the cue ball into the object ball on the right-hand side, banking it into the lower cushion (Diagram 34). This is a speed shot. You need to make sure that the object ball stays on the cushion so it doesn't end up in front of a pocket. The cue ball is struck with high right English. The end result is that the object ball ends up hidden behind the two other balls. Even if you fail to snooker your opponent, all you have left is a very difficult bank shot.

SITUATION #2.   Just shoot a stop shot, hitting the cue ball dead center. The object ball will go to the opposite rail while the cue ball is blocked (preferably even touching) the other ball (Diagram 35).

SITUATIONS #3 AND #4.   These are not snookers (as were the two previous examples), but they are good safeties.

SITUATION #3.   You're faced with an eight ball that can't be pocketed in the side and there are no other easy shots on the table. Hit the cue ball with some low left English, being sure to keep it in the upper part of the table, and bank the eight into the cushion close to the other side and end of the table (Diagram 36). You leave your opponent with a l-o-n-g bank shot—which we don't mind. And even if he makes the eight, the nine will be on the rail at the other end of the table.

SITUATION #4.   Only the nine ball is left, but you don't want to risk that long bank. This safety is a speed shot made with center-to-high English. Bank the nine to go straight across the table to the other side while the cue ball stays down on the other side of the table (Diagram 37).

Let your opponent try that bank.

Object Ball

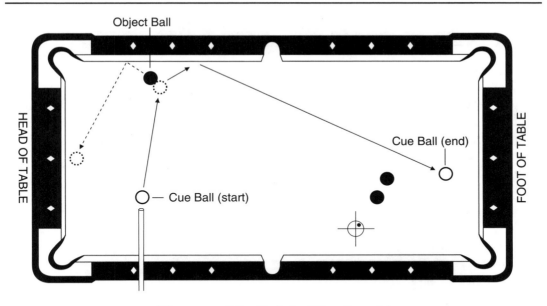

Diagram 34: Safety Situation #1

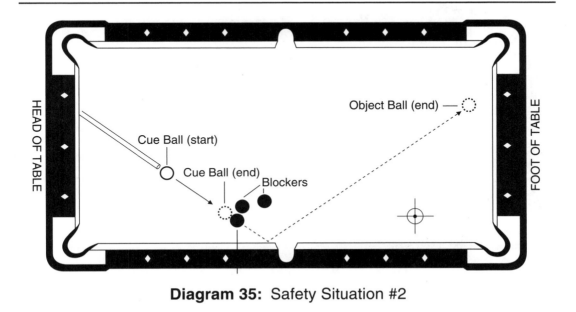

Diagram 35: Safety Situation #2

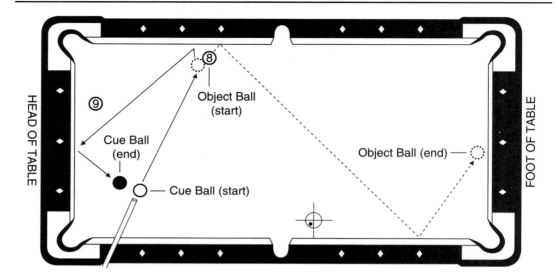

Diagram 36: Safety Situation #3

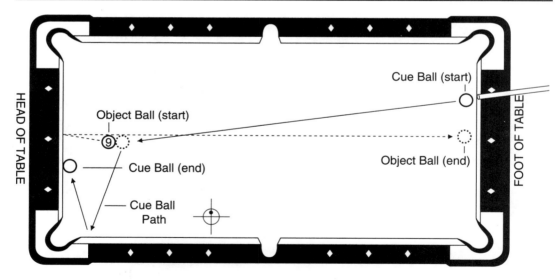

Diagram 37: Safety Situation #4

7

Eight Ball

$\mathcal{E}$ight ball is unquestionably the most popular pool game in the United States. It's played in leagues throughout the country, in bars, in colleges, everywhere. It's also known by its nickname: "stripes and solids."

It is a great beginner's game.

Unlike nine ball, in which you are restricted to shooting at a specific ball, immediately after the break in eight ball (assuming no balls were pocketed) each player has fifteen possible shots from which to choose.

And then, of course, it all comes down to that big black ball sitting on the table. Sink the eight ball last, and no matter how the game was played, you have won!

BREAK

In eight ball you are dealing with a full rack on every break, and fifteen balls—sixteen, counting the cue ball, will be rolling all over the table.

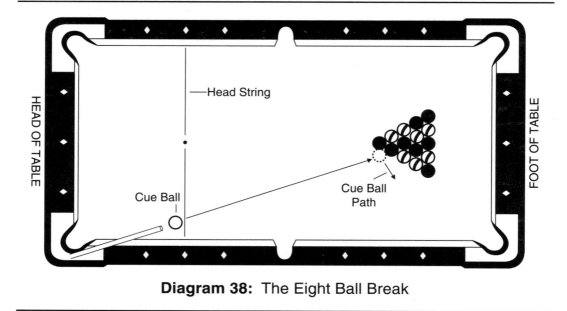

Diagram 38: The Eight Ball Break

Your power break shot should be aimed at the second tier of balls, not the head ball in the rack unless "house rules" require that you hit the head ball first, so check. You will find that the balls consistently disperse better if you hit the second row. Hit the cue ball with low English, just enough to assure that you do not scratch in the corner pocket (Diagram 38).

It is vital to play position on the one in a nine ball break, but in eight ball the requirement is not as stringent, so you can pretty much whale away and see what happens.

PATTERNS

Patterning in eight ball has somewhat different requirements than in nine ball. It is important to look ahead, your first task is to identify the nasty situations on the table: clusters of balls that will have to be broken up, balls lying close to the cushions, frozen balls, and so on.

You need to get to the problems as soon as possible, before too many of your balls have been pocketed.

And just because eight ball presents you with myriad shot opportunities, you should not assume that the best pattern will not include a safety. If you consciously play toward a safety, you can not only leave your opponent with a difficult shot but, often, you can force him to take a shot that will ease the way for you later in the game. You can force him to disturb a ball that left alone would create problems for you.

It works the other way as well. If you have a "hanger" (a ball almost on the lip of the pocket), leave it alone for as long as you can. It will block that pocket and force your opponent to play on a table that, essentially, has only five pockets.

If anything, you have to form your pattern even farther ahead in eight ball. You have more leeway in the intermediate shots, but your pattern must take the eight ball into account from the very start. The eight is your key ball. If you run seven balls only to discover that the eight ball can't be pocketed, all your hard work was a waste.

While the eight is very definitely the key ball, you should also try to pinpoint a secondary key ball—the ball that will give you clean access to the eight for the final shot. The worst thing that could happen is for you to run your balls off, only to miss the eight ball, leaving your opponent in control even if all his balls are still on the table. Chances of the game ending up in your favor at that point are slim to none.

EIGHT BALL PLAY

The first important choice you are faced with in eight ball after the break is selecting which series of balls to choose: stripes or solids. Look for the layout that has the least amount of problems and where there are "help" balls that can assist you in solving the puzzle. Here are a couple of examples.

SITUATION #1. Choose the solids and leave the A ball for two reasons: it is a key ball for the eight and it blocks the corner pocket (Diagram 39).

SITUATION #2. Choose the "stripes" because the A ball will allow you to easily break up that cluster (Diagram 40).

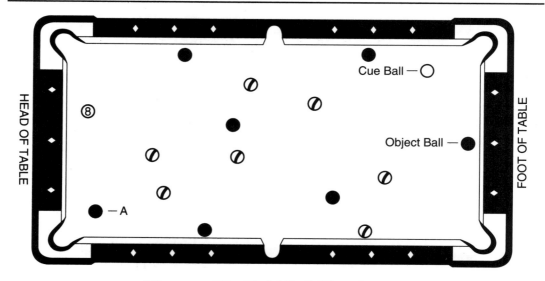

Diagram 39: Eight Ball Situation #1

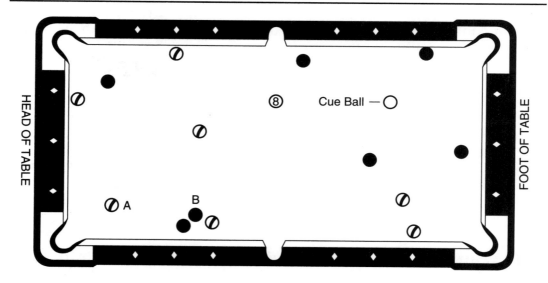

Diagram 40: Eight Ball Situation #2

Let's go through an eight ball pattern.

SITUATION #3. Use center right English when you sink the one ball (Diagram 41). That will cause the cue ball to go two cushions and offer you a shot at the same pocket with the two.

SITUATION #4. Pocket the two with a stop shot, giving you position on the three in the side (Diagram 42).

SITUATION #5. Pocket the three and drift down using low center English for the four (Diagram 43).

SITUATION #6. Make the four and draw the cue back for the five, leaving an angle to easily get to the eight (Diagram 44).

SITUATION #7. Cut the five in and bring the cue ball over with high English for a shot on the eight into the same corner (Diagram 45).

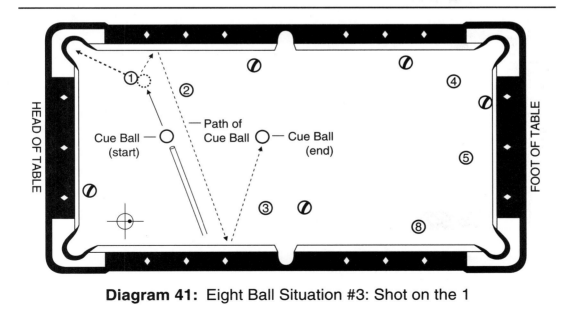

Diagram 41: Eight Ball Situation #3: Shot on the 1

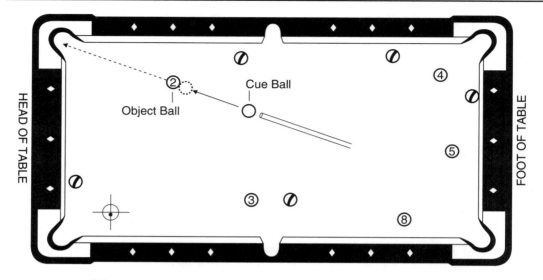

Diagram 42: Eight Ball Situation #4: Shot on the 2

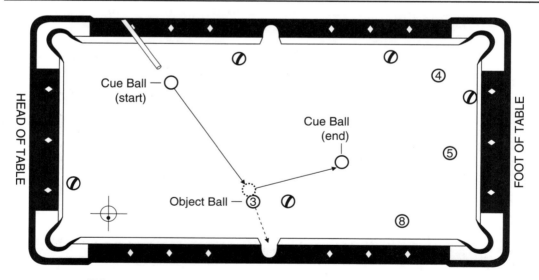

Diagram 43: Eight Ball Situation #5: Shot on the 3

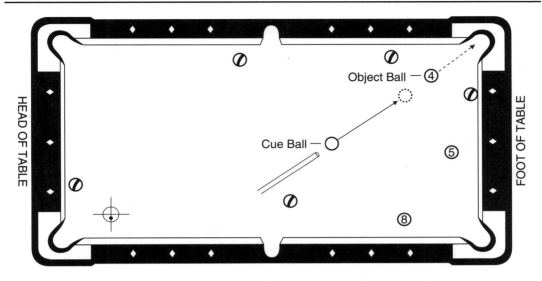

Diagram 44: Eight Ball Situation #6: Shot on the 4

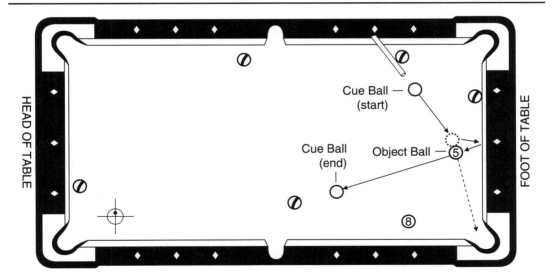

Diagram 45: Eight Ball Situation #7: Shot on the 5

8

Straight Pool

*T*his is the game I was brought up on. The key is control. You must always play the percentages, making sure that you never leave an open shot for your opponent if you must stop your run.

In straight pool, the action can continue for a run of 40, 50, or 100 balls. The late Willie Mosconi, if not the greatest player ever, then surely one of them, once pocketed 526 consecutive balls! The reason such runs can occur in this game is because you can choose to call any ball on the table. You're not restricted to the solids or the stripes as you are in eight ball, or to the next numerical ball as you are in nine ball. This is the game that offers you the most leeway — and therefore the most need — to see and create your own patterns.

But we're getting ahead of ourselves. Let's start at the beginning with the opening break — or the opening safety, as is usually the case.

THE OPENING BREAK

Because you have to designate what ball is going to fall into which pocket, the opening break in straight pool is distinctly different from the one in eight ball or nine ball. The odds are very long that any player, even an accomplished one, can correctly call a specific ball

84

out of a rack. And the penalty is daunting. Not only do you lose your turn, but you turn over a wide-open table to your opponent. So, instead of trying to break the balls open with a power shot, the opening break in straight pool is a defensive one designed to prevent the other player from getting a clean, callable shot. The opening break tests a player's tactical ability, knowledge of English, touch . . . and patience.

Let's go through the opening break situation to illustrate what I mean. Even before I set up for the shot, I double-check to see that the rack is tight, so that there is no possibility that any balls will come flying out of the rack unexpectedly.

After I've checked the rack, I spot the cue ball almost on the head string and straight out from the first diamond on the end rail. I want to make a very thin cut on the outside ball in the rack, with just a bit of right-hand spin on the cue ball so that it will follow the path shown in Diagram 46 and end up back down near the end rail—on the rail, if possible.

Ideally, the two outside balls in the rack (A and B) will go out to the cushions and carom back toward the rack (Diagram 47). Even if they do not, as long as you position the cue ball back down on the end rail,

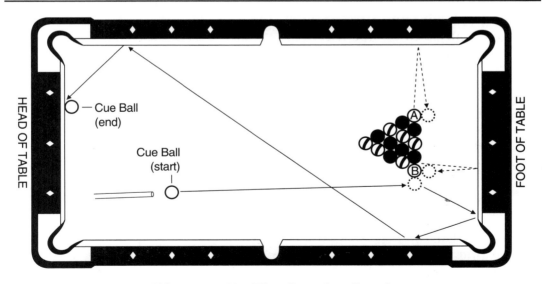

Diagram 46: The Opening Break

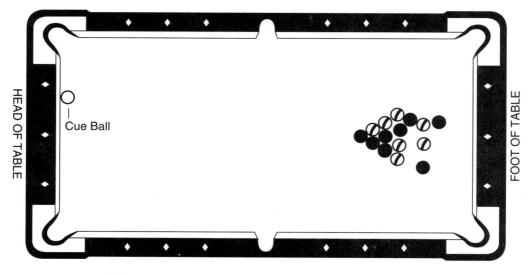

Diagram 47: Results of the Opening Break

you have left your opponent with a shot that is very difficult. It almost demands that he play a safety. That is the secret of the opening break: cue ball control, not just the thin cut but also the ability to leave the cue ball where you want it.

SAFETIES

Okay, the opening shot has been made, and let's say that now you are the second player. Again, you check the rack, and this time you should also be looking for balls that are lined straight for a pocket or dead-cinch combinations on a ball aligned straight into a pocket. Any time the balls have been moved, you should do this, just in case.

Nothing is there, so next you look for the right ball to hit for a safety. That is the ball that is least likely to drive any other balls into position for a good shot for your opponent. In Diagram 48 you have a good candidate, a ball that is slightly loose from the rack and has little chance of setting up another ball even if it hits one softly. You call a "safety" ball, and hit that ball super, super thin. But preferably, you should have

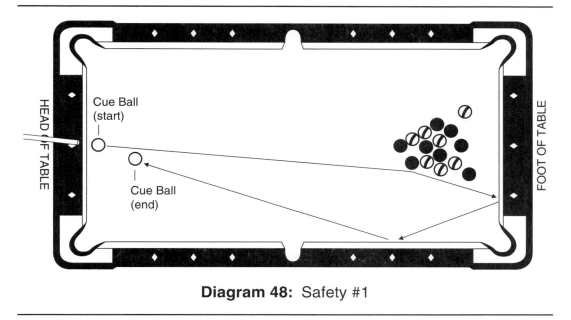

Diagram 48: Safety #1

enough speed on the cue ball so that it will come off the cushions and leave your opponent a long shot from the opposite end rail.

One of the first considerations on any safety is to leave your opponent as tough a shot as possible. Sometimes this means leaving him down on the end rail and in a position that you hope will force him to leave you a better shot. Another defensive alternative is to freeze the cue ball to the cluster, leaving no open shot (Diagram 49). Go ahead and be creative, just don't hand it over! Sometimes you may be better off playing a safety even if there is a good shot on the table. In Diagram 50, the lone ball on the rail is very makable, but where would sinking it leave you? Because the rest of the balls are tied up, you're better off calling a safety, pocketing the ball anyway and having it put back up on the foot spot for your opponent to deal with. You're giving up one point to potentially gain a bunch.

There are times when you may have no shot at all, or when your only shot may present your opponent with a good opportunity to do some damage. This is the time to take an intentional foul. By not driving a ball to a cushion after contact, you commit a foul and lose a point. Here is a common situation where it is extremely difficult to get a thin

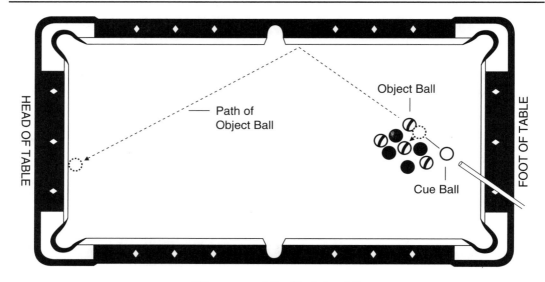

Diagram 49: Safety #2

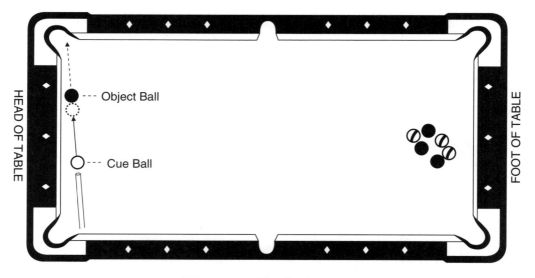

Diagram 50: Safety #3

enough cut on any ball and not leave a shot. Simply roll the cue ball with moderate speed to the end cushion and into the stack (Diagram 51). The idea is to knock only a couple of balls out. Beware of hitting this shot too hard, so the balls don't come out and leave your opponent some kind of shot. You may again lose a point, but at least you didn't hand anything over, and you'll have an entirely new look at the table when you return. Never give up!

Here are a couple of examples of full rack safeties. In this situation the break ball has already been pocketed. Play the cue ball directly into ball A with center English. The idea is for the cue ball to stick to the rack and also to knock a couple of balls out to make it more difficult for the other player to shoot safely.

Diagram 53 presents a similar rack safe. Using a soft to medium stroke, roll the cue ball up to ball B just hard enough for a ball to reach a cushion.

Something to keep in mind when you're looking at these shots is that the angle *must* be such that you can hit a full ball straight on. Hit just a little bit off to either side and you will leave a dream rack for your opponent.

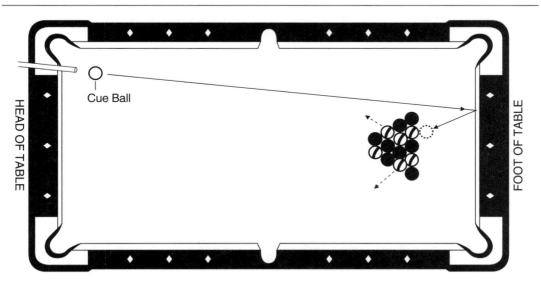

Diagram 51: Safety #4

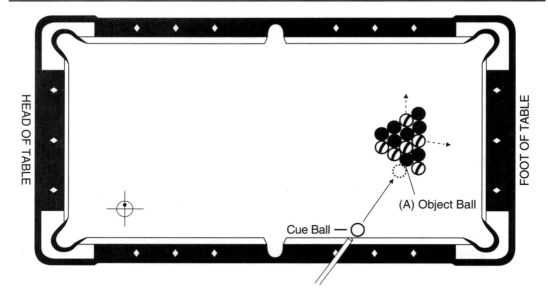

Diagram 52: Safety #5

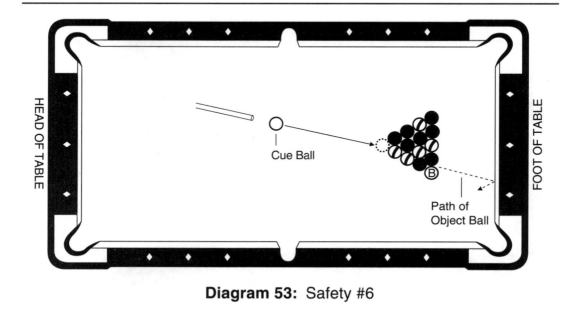

Diagram 53: Safety #6

BREAK SHOTS

These are primarily what separates straight pool from the other games. It is played continuously, unlike nine ball, for example, in which you stop between racks, rerack, and begin a new game. In straight pool you must create your own break shots. Diagrams *54 to 57* will show you some of the most popular ones.

Diagram 54 presents the break with which you will have the most control of the cue ball. Irving Crane, one of the legends of pool, would mostly look for a break shot similar to this one, where he could pocket the ball, have the cue ball go into the top ball of the rack, and nudge a few balls out. Shoot with a little low left English to draw the cue ball out to the center of the table, where the odds are the best that you'll have a clear shot after the break.

Next is a similar shot, only the object ball is positioned lower, so that after contact with the object ball the cue ball cannot hit the top ball in the rack. Play this instead to hit the bottom ball with high English (Diagram 55). The balls will spread nicely, and again try to get

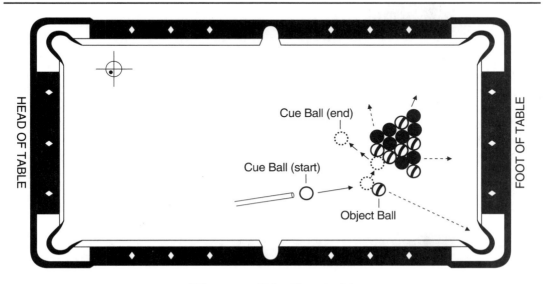

Diagram 54: Break #1

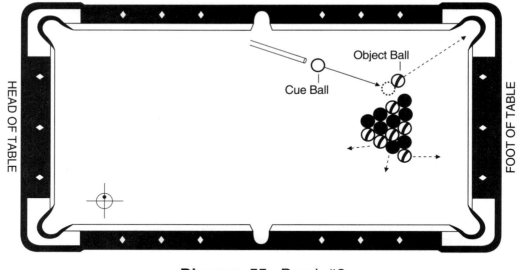

Diagram 55: Break #2

the cue ball back up to somewhere in the middle of the table. Note that in both of these shots the idea is to hit one of the corner balls. Try not to hit one in the middle of the pack, or chances are you will get stuck there. There is too much resistance from the weight of the full rack to let the cue ball run through. Again, looking to hit the corner ball after making the break shot, hit this with some high left English and with enough speed to pocket the ball, disturb the rack, and have the cue ball return to the center (Diagram 56).

The last break is a bit more risky because controlling the cue ball enough to make sure it does not hit the full rack is more difficult than the previous shots, but it is still a legitimate and good break shot, and there are dozens more (Diagram 57). So be creative! Remember, once you get the break down, you may run hundreds!

PATTERNS

Now that we have an understanding of break shots, it is time to back up a bit and figure out how we're going to play the table in order even

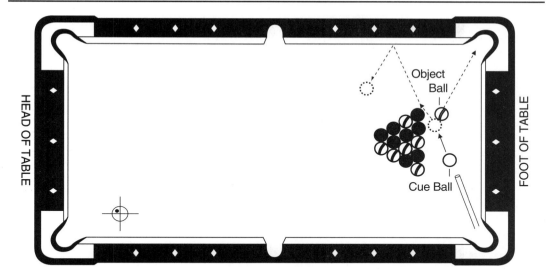

Diagram 56: Break #3

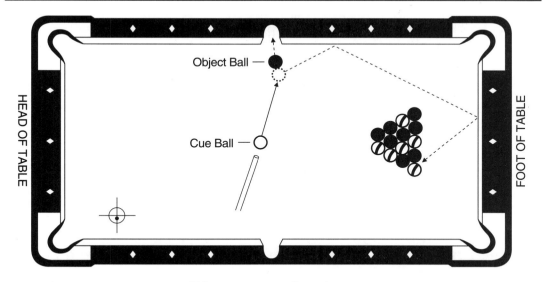

Diagram 57: Break #4

to have an opportunity to attempt a break. And you do that by patterning your shot-making opportunities toward the break.

The reason straight pool is also known as "fourteen point one" is that you pocket fourteen balls then have one ball left to shoot in and, at the same time, begin the next rack. The name implies—rightfully—that the break ball is played differently.

You'll hear a lot of players who have just had their runs stopped, complaining that it was just a matter of rotten luck, that they made a great break shot but didn't get a shot afterward. Mosconi didn't make 526 balls by luck. He was a master at positioning the cue ball and the break ball to assure himself of shots after the break.

You might not have the talent of Mosconi, but I will give you a system that will help you create the patterns that will sustain your run. It is a way of thinking and planning that will give you the greatest number of shot opportunities. And it's simple, requiring only six basic steps:

1. Examine the table layout. Pick out the trouble balls. Find the balls frozen on a rail, the clusters that must be broken up, the ball isolated at one end of the table, and so on. Don't forget that some clusters are no problem if you pocket one or two balls around it, opening paths for the other balls into the pockets.

2. Make your shot selection based on eliminating those trouble balls. This does not mean you shoot at those balls immediately. But you should be on the lookout for makable shots that also offer potential to move the trouble balls.

3. Identify a break ball. In straight pool, the key to continuing your run is, of course, the break ball, but also look for a "key ball," a ball that will allow you to easily get to the break ball. As soon as you can, identify a ball in a good area of the table near the rack that you can use for the next break shot and a key ball to get to it.

4. Establish a three- or four-ball pattern leading into the break shot. You have fifteen balls to sink between break shots, and there is no one pattern to follow. You have to create that. You should be able to eliminate the trouble balls by midway to three quarters of the way through the rack, and then you can concentrate on playing a pattern of shots that will wind up with the cue ball in perfect position to pocket the break ball and open the rack.

5. Be willing to change your pattern. There's a lot of action on the table during straight pool. Balls are moving all the time. You may be forced to change your pattern or your break ball at some point— in some games, it seems that you have to on almost every shot. That's simply the nature of straight pool. Don't be surprised, just be ready to change.

6. Pocket your shots. You can have the greatest pattern in the world, but you'll never get to play it if you don't concentrate on sinking the object ball.

By now you should have a pretty good idea of basic patterning from the preceding chapters on eight ball and nine ball. There's no sense in repeating all that. Instead, here's an example of how to put those elements together in straight pool, where every ball—not just a specific few or a single one—is a potential shot opportunity. We'll assume you've been playing well and have already run nine balls from this rack.

The break ball we have chosen is "X." A properly played corner shot will send the cue ball into the next rack. Working backward so that you will have a good angle on the "X" as your final shot for this rack, you may come up with this sequence (Diagrams 58 to 63):

- Shoot the one ball into the corner and come back out for position on the two.

- Sink the two in the opposite corner, draw the cue ball back for a nearly straight shot on the three.

- The three is pocketed in the corner and all you have to do is use a bit of a draw for position on the four in the side.

- Sink the four in the side, with a full stop shot.

- Cut the five into the corner pocket and have the cue ball come out a bit. Rack 'em.

- A perfect angle shot off the break ball (X) into the rack.

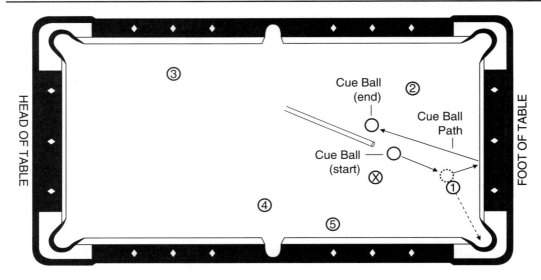

Diagram 58: Shot on the 1

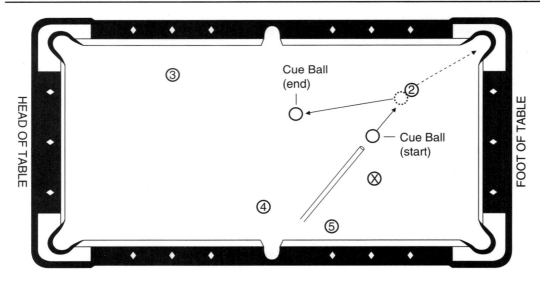

Diagram 59: Shot on the 2

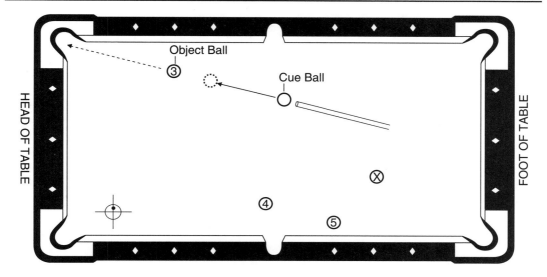

Diagram 60: Shot on the 3

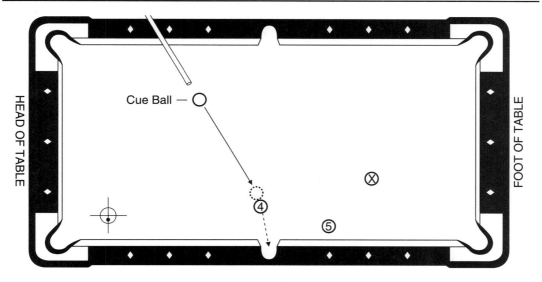

Diagram 61: Shot on the 4

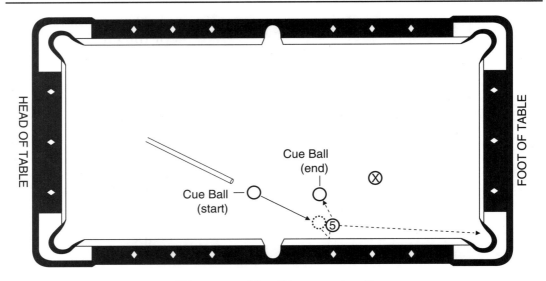

Diagram 62: Shot on the 5

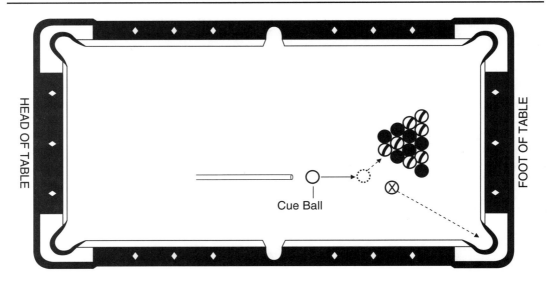

Diagram 63: Shot on the Break Ball

Nicely done. You made it easy on yourself, made the cue ball move around as little as possible, and, all the while, kept the cue ball on the correct side of the object ball so that you had no problem playing position on any subsequent shot.

Before we leave straight pool I want to underline the fact that it is a game of defense as well as offense. You must play your opponent as well as the table. It may sound like a contradiction, but because straight pool is a wide-open game, I find myself playing it conservatively. In most cases I will play it safe rather than go for a low-percentage shot. You can't afford to give your opponent an opening. Play a Houdini shot in nine ball and, even if you miss, you may leave your opponent with a bad shot because you know what ball he must shoot at. Straight pool isn't so forgiving. Your opponent has a table full of balls to play. Leave one open and you may not even get a chance to escape.

Practice Handbook

*I*n other chapters I have suggested drills to help or analyze specific techniques. Here are some general practice drills that will help keep any player sharp. At first they may be difficult. Stick with them. It's not like having to do twenty-five stomach crunches followed by twenty-five leg crossovers every day. Believe me, I know how quickly that repetitive stuff becomes boring. These are some of the drills I practice.

EXERCISE #1

Line up a series of balls perpendicular to the end cushion. Place the cue ball a few inches away and on an angle for a cut shot into the corner pocket (Diagram 64). Make the first ball into the corner pocket, using the cushion to play position.

Do not touch the cue ball. Use English and speed to position the cue ball for each successive shot, leaving yourself a similar angle on the next ball. Not only will you be developing your ability to use English, but you will see that speed plays an important role in your success at running the entire series of balls.

100

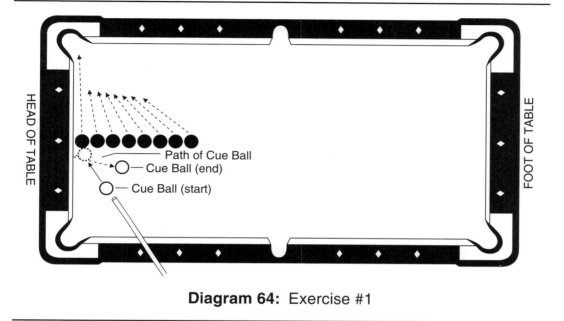

Diagram 64: Exercise #1

Turn the whole drill around and shoot at the opposite corner pocket.

EXERCISE #2

Line up a series of balls on an angle in front of a corner pocket, this time avoiding the cushion. Use draw to bring the cue ball back and in position for each successive shot, constantly staying on the left side of the ball for each shot (Diagram 65).

EXERCISE #3

Align the balls to form a letter *L* in front of a corner pocket. Sink them in order (Diagram 66). Again, you cannot touch the cue ball. But you

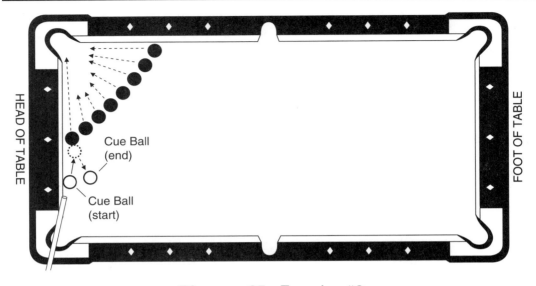

Diagram 65: Exercise #2

---

can either draw the cue ball straight back or use the cushions to position the cue ball for the next shot.

All three of these drills will improve your control of the cue ball and add to your confidence.

EXERCISE #4

This drill presents a challenge while practicing speed and English.

Place a target anywhere on the table—something like a cocktail napkin makes a good target. The idea is to have the cue ball stop on the target after pocketing a shot (Diagram 67). It can be almost any shot, but it should be makable according to your skill level.

I've illustrated a fairly simple corner cut shot with the target nearly centered on the table (see diagram). Once you can hit that target fairly regularly, move it. Or you can change the position of the ball you have to pocket. The possibilities are almost infinite.

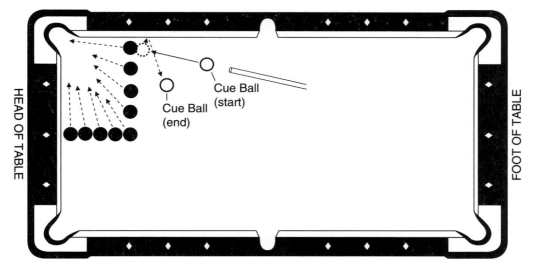

Diagram 66: Exercise #3

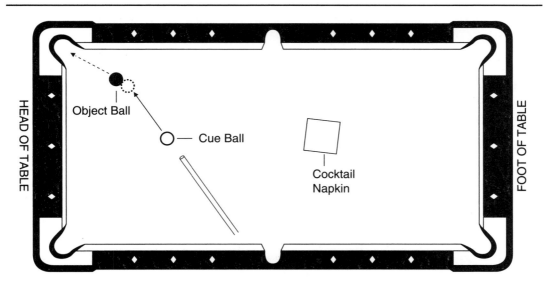

Diagram 67: Exercise #4

EXERCISE #5

This is one of my favorites. It is an effective way to demonstrate what happens to the cue ball after contact with other balls. To underline that, scatter the object balls around the table and try to pocket them by shooting them off the cue ball (Diagram 68). In other words, you are reversing the way a shot is normally taken. In the illustration, you will try to shoot the object ball off the cue ball and into the side pocket. I find this to be an excellent way to improve your understanding of billiards and your position play as well.

EXERCISE #6

Line up a series of balls close to the side rail opposite you and bank them into the side pocket nearest to you (Diagram 69). This will help you understand and refresh yourself on the effects of English and speed on bank shots.

These are the type of banks that you're "supposed" to make, but that does not mean they don't require their fair share of practice. Try shooting them with different speed and English to really get an understanding of how much that can affect a bank shot. Learn how to use both to your advantage. (See "Bank Shots" on page 49).

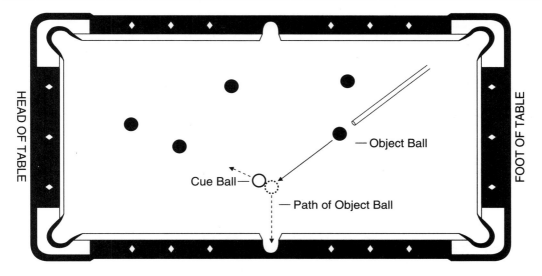

Diagram 68: Exercise #5

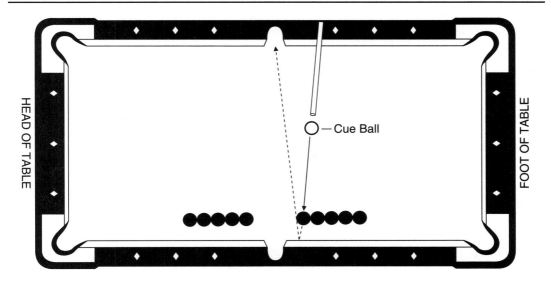

Diagram 69: Exercise #6

10

Trick Shots

$\mathcal{P}$ool should, above all, be fun. We have been going at it pretty heavy, so let's take a break and learn some shots that have been created just to dazzle. Trick shots are kind of like the big rocket barrage at the end of the fireworks display—lots of flash, lots of sparkle, a few surprises.

These shots may take some work to learn, but believe me, the reaction you will get makes it worth it.

Here's a collection of my personal favorite trick shots. Have fun!

THE EVEL KNEIVEL

This commemorates the most famous motorcycle daredevil of them all. It is a spectacular jump shot (Diagram 70).

- Place a ball (A) on the foot spot. Freeze another ball (B) aimed at the right corner pocket. (They must be touching.)

- At the other end of the table place the cue ball and line up six balls in front of it in double file. These balls must be close enough together that the cue ball cannot pass between them.

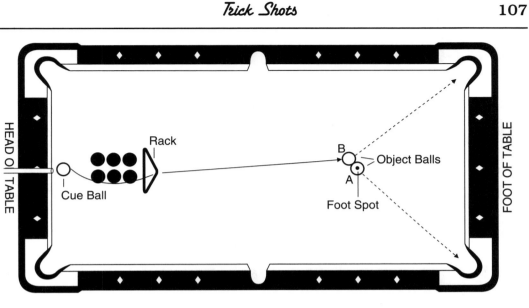

Diagram 70: The Evel Kneivel

- Place the rack, standing on end, in front of the double row of balls.

- Aim a jump shot for ball B.

- Evel (the cue ball) will jump over the six balls, through the triangle and sink ball B in the left-hand corner while ball A goes straight into the right corner.

FASTER THAN THE EYE

Play this one on someone who is not familiar with the game.

- Line up the cue ball and ball B straight into the corner pocket (Diagram 71).

- Place A between the other two balls. One third of A should be in the line of aim between the cue ball and ball B.

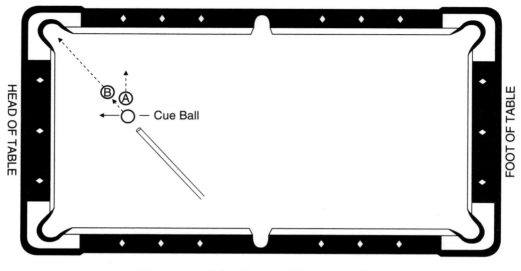

Diagram 71: Faster Than the Eye

- Shoot the cue ball into A and exaggerate your follow-through so that the tip of the cue stick strikes ball B, sending it into the corner.

- Hey, it's a foul, but if you do this quickly enough, no one will know. (P. S. This is only for trick shots...)

CLEAR THE TABLE

This belongs in the "stroke shot" category.

- Put the cue ball (A) in front of the right-hand corner of the side pocket.

- Freeze ball B, aimed at the left side of the other side pocket.

- Freeze ball C, aimed toward the first diamond.

- Place ball D at the corner pocket on the opposite rail.

- Place the eight ball (E) near the corner pocket nearest you at the opposite rail (Diagram 72).

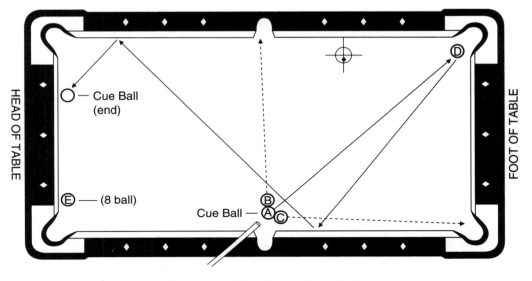

Diagram 72: Clear the Table

- Shoot the cue ball to sink ball D. Use extreme draw.

- Balls B and C will "throw" into the side and corner pockets.

A great visual effect occurs when the cue ball "stops" as it sinks ball D and then comes shooting back to the cushion near you and caroms down to the opposite rail, leaving it in position to sink the eight.

Now, don't blow the deal by goofing up on the eight.

THE COLOR OF MONEY

If you saw the movie *The Color of Money*, you probably remember this shot that Tom Cruise used to put away an opponent.

- Freeze the cue ball to ball A. They should be lined up straight down the table.

- Place the nine ball within the jaws of the corner pocket.

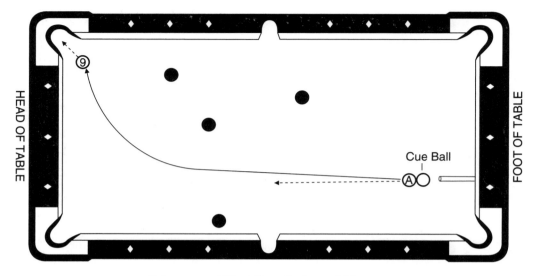

Diagram 73: The Color of Money

- Scatter several balls similar to Diagram 73, leaving a path for the nine.

- Elevate the back of the cue stick and hit down with extreme right-hand spin.

- The cue ball will start out straight ahead, then curve dramatically to the right and will sink the nine. It may take a few tries before you find what is the right amount of speed and spin.

- Show big, toothy grin.

THE MIDDLEDITCH

This one is named after George Middleditch, a good friend who invented this amazing shot.

- Place a ball (B) in front of the corner pocket at one end of the table.

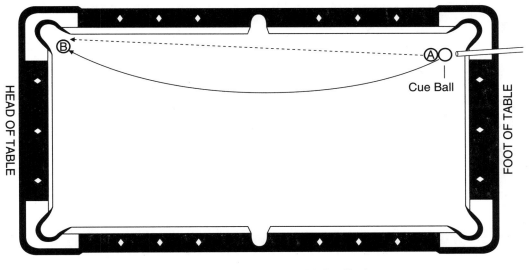

Diagram 74: The Middleditch

- Freeze the cue ball and ball A together at the other end of the table, aimed at the third diamond (Diagram 74).

- Elevate the back of your cue stick and with high right-hand English shoot down on the cue ball with extreme follow-through.

- The cue ball will actually pass ball A and go on to pocket ball B ...

- ... and then ball A will come rolling down the table and fall into the same pocket.

THE RAILROAD

This is one of the most famous trick shots of all time. The first time I ever saw it, the late Willie Mosconi made it. He then taught it to me in Atlantic City in 1982. I think that is why it is my favorite.

- Line up balls A and B on the left side of the side pocket (they must be straight and frozen).

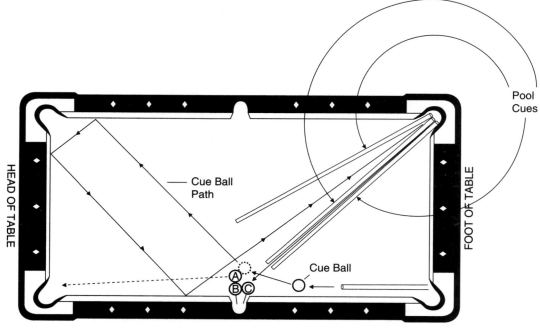

Diagram 75: The Railroad

- Place ball C at the opposite side of the same pocket.

- Place the cue ball just off the rail behind ball C (Diagram 75).

- Find three straight house cues of the same length. Line up two of them side by side, with their grip ends at the corner pocket so that their tips are aimed directly at ball C (they must be even).

- Place the grip end of the third cue at the same pocket, but open it up so that the tip is about a foot from the tips of the other two cues.

- Aim the cue ball at the first diamond on the far rail.

- Hit the cue ball with high left-hand English.

Stand back and watch the cue ball send A into the corner, B into the side, go three rails around, and—if it was hit with the correct speed—swoop around the corner pocket and "ride the rails" (the two side-by-side cues) and sink C.

Spectacular!

11

The Women's Side

*W*hile this is a guide to pool intended for all players, male or female, and I have no intention of sneaking in a polemic, I feel strongly that I should at least acknowledge my feminine predecessors in the game.

According to noted billiards historian Michael Ian Shamos, billiards has existed in a form that would be recognizable to contemporary players for about five centuries. It was assumed that in its very early days billiards was a pastime exclusively of the idle nobility. That might not be entirely correct, and there is evidence that the game was far more democratic, played by peasants (in the precious little spare time they might find) and nobility alike—and played by men and women of all classes.

Of course, court historians and artists were not about to waste much time recording and illuminating the diversions of the lower classes—after all, think about who paid their salaries—so most evidence of the game records only how it was conducted in the upper realms of society. One of the best known instances is that while imprisoned and awaiting execution, Mary Queen of Scots was allowed to play billiards by Queen Elizabeth I (who herself much enjoyed the game). This anecdote loses some of its historical charm when one learns that following Mary's beheading in 1587 her corpse was wrapped in the cloth taken from her billiards table.

While men and women might have played the game together, it would not be accurate to say that they played as true equals. Women, for instance, were required to use a "mace" (something like a scaled-down shuffleboard stick) instead of a cue stick until about the middle of the nineteenth century. Nevertheless, that same era represented an early high point in the game's acceptance, as it was often taught to young ladies in finishing schools. Queen Victoria had a pool table, and by the end of the century, so did all the truly fashionable ladies of America, including Mrs. John Jacob Astor (and, therefore, one assumes the Vanderbilts as well).

But even as pool was taken up as a fad by the noble and very rich, the Industrial Revolution had provided all levels of society with more leisure time. Pool tables began to show up in public houses, taverns, and even in special halls built for the game. Table time could be rented by nearly anyone. And the game began to acquire a somewhat rakish image. Remember that this was an era when a glimpse of stocking was regarded as something shocking. And in such a context, the postures required of pool players were certainly shocking. Illustrators of magazine articles and publishers of "postcards" frequently used pool as a theme for their "saucy" material. I never cease to be amazed at how many behind-the-back shots women took in those days.

Offsetting that was the fact that individual female players were earning worldwide respect for their ability. Grace Fairweather and Ella Collins staged the first woman's championship in England in 1897. Alice Howard gave lecture tours and demonstrations and wrote prolifically on the game in the early part of this century. May Kaarlus, who was Flemish, became internationally famous not only as a player but for her dazzling trick shot ability—she was unparalleled at the time and would be a standout even today.

In the United States, Bertha May King was almost unbeatable in women's competitions from around 1915 to the late 1920s. But probably better known were the Flower sisters, Florence and Maud, who parlayed their tournament wins into a popular vaudeville act. Clara Katherine Heywood may have been the best of them all, often playing top male players head up and winning. Her international counterpart was Lies Schrier of Holland, who broke the sex barrier in the 1924 European Championships (a similar honor was never accorded Heywood in the United States).

By mid-century, Ruth McGinnis became the women's standard-bearer in America, where she toured with and played against the top male pros. Diminutive Masako Katsura (five feet tall, ninety-six pounds), was unbeatable in billiards in her native Japan for almost two decades surrounding World War II. She eventually married an American airman, and in the early 1950s was invited to play in world championship tournaments against the likes of Willie Hoppe and Irving Crane—she remains the only woman to have been so honored.

More recently, the luminaries have included Dorothy Wise, who won the U.S. Open pocket billiards championship the first five years it was held (1967 through 1971), and the controversial Jean Balukas. Balukas seemed destined to become a superstar in the 1970s as she mowed down competition and was often seen on television. After dominating the women's field for years, she abruptly retired from competition in 1989.

Which brings us to the contemporary scene. The average level of women's tournament play is at an all-time high. The field in every major women's professional tournament has depth, so that competition is close right from first-round play. Blowout games are the rarity rather than the rule nowadays.

If this is not the golden age of women's pool, I predict that the age has dawned. With over forty million people playing the game today, and about a third of those being women, we can't go anywhere but forward. The Women's Professional Billiard Association (WPBA), which was started in 1976 by a few female pros, has grown far beyond anyone's expectations. The year 1993 was a banner one for the women as they took matters even more into their own hands. With Harold Simonsen, publisher of *Pool & Billiard Magazine*; Shari Stauch, secretary of the WPBA; Vicki Paski, president and the tour coordinator; and Peg Ledman at the forefront, the WPBA Classic Billiard Tour was formed. With tremendous support from the billiard industry and the tireless work of the players themselves, professional women's pool is flourishing like never before.

Equally important is the industry's involvement in amateur and junior billiards in America and abroad, opening the doors for more and more people to be able to enjoy this great game.

Glossary

$\mathcal{E}$very sport develops its own jargon. Pool is no exception. Here is my own personal short list of words and phrases that will get you started in speaking "pool."

Ball-in-hand—When, after a foul, a player is allowed to position the cue ball anywhere on the table.

Bank—Rebound a ball off a cushion.

Diamond—Inlaid indicator set in the top of the rails that is useful in determining caroms and banks.

Combination—Cue ball strikes an object ball that, in turn, strikes a second object ball.

Carom—Cue ball strikes the object ball and then continues on to strike a second object ball.

Cheese—Winning ball.

Cue ball—White ball that always is struck first.

Felt—Fabric covering the playing surface.

Dog it — "Choking"; particularly, missing the winning ball.

English — Various spins you put on the cue ball.

Ferrule — Collar that is placed between the shaft and the leather tip of the cue.

Foot of the table — End of the table where the balls are racked.

Foot spot — Precise point on the table where the head ball in a rack must be placed for the break.

Foul — Illegal shot; for example, a failure to contact the object ball or scratching in a pocket.

Freeze — Two (or more) balls in contact, or a ball touching a rail.

George — Almost incredible feat, situation, shot, feeling.

Hanger — Easy shot; ball on the very edge of a pocket.

Head of the table — End of the table from which the break is made.

Head string/Head spot — Imaginary line on the table behind which the cue ball must be positioned for the break.

In stroke — Playing well.

Jump — Cue ball actually leaves the bed of the table.

Kitchen — Area behind the head string.

Massé — Extreme curve (applied spin) on the cue ball.

Lag — Process to determine which player will break. Balls are banked table-length. The player positioning his ball closest to the head rail wins.

The Nuts — When you "can't lose"; you're on a roll.

Pocket — (n.) Openings at each corner of the table and midway in the side rails; (v.) Sink a ball into one of the pockets.

Position — Plan where the cue ball will stop for succeeding shots.

Push out — In nine ball, immediately following the break, the first incoming player is allowed to "push" the cue ball anywhere he wants, with the opponent having a choice as to shoot or to ask the first player to shoot again.

Rack — Wood or plastic triangle used to precisely align the balls for the break shot.

Rails — Sides of the table on which the fabric-covered cushions surrounding the playing surface are mounted. Also the cushions themselves.

Rotation — Playing the balls in numerical order.

Safety — When, after a legal hit, the balls are positioned in a manner that is disadvantageous to the incoming player; i.e., to create a snooker.

Scratch — Inadvertently pocketing the cue ball.

Shape — Play position; that is, you "play shape."

Snooker — Leave the cue ball so it is blocked from the object ball.

"Solids" — Balls one through seven.

"Stripes" — Balls nine through fifteen.

Stripes and solids — Game of eight ball.

Sweater — Person who will watch any pool game, anywhere, anytime.

Whitey — Cue ball.

Wrap — Handle of the cue stick.

Rules

$\mathcal{I}$ thought it would be a good idea to include the rules for the three major games whether you are just learning how to play or need to look up a rule judgment. Courtesy of the Billiard Congress of America, these are the official rules of most professional and amateur events in the United States.

EIGHT BALL

STANDARDIZED WORLD RULES

Except when clearly contradicted by these additional rules, the General Rules of Pocket Billiards apply.

Object of the Game. Eight Ball is a call shot game played with a cue ball and fifteen object balls, numbered 1 through 15. One player must pocket balls of the group numbered 1 through 7 (solid colors), while the other player has 9 through 15 (stripes). THE PLAYER POCKETING HIS GROUP FIRST AND THEN LEGALLY POCKETING THE 8-BALL WINS THE GAME.

Call Shot. In Call Shot, obvious balls and pockets do not have to be indicated. It is the opponent's right to ask which ball and pocket if he is unsure of the shot. Bank shots and combination shots are not considered obvious, and care should be taken in calling both the object ball and the intended pocket. When calling the shot, it is NEVER necessary to indicate details such as the number of cushions, banks, kisses, caroms, etc. Any balls pocketed on a foul remain pocketed, regardless of whether they belong to the shooter or the opponent.

The opening break is not a "called shot." Any player performing a break shot in Eight Ball may continue to shoot his next shot so long as he has legally pocketed any object ball on the break.

Racking the Balls. The balls are racked in a triangle at the foot of the table with the 8-ball in the center of the triangle, the first ball of the rack on the foot spot, a stripe ball in one corner of the rack and a solid ball in the other corner.

Alternating Break. Winner of the lag has the option to break. During individual competition, players will alternate breaking on each subsequent game.

Jump and Massé Shot Foul. While "cue ball fouls only" is the rule of play when a match is not presided over by a referee, a player should be aware that it will be considered a cue ball foul if during an attempt to jump, curve or massé the cue ball over or around an impeding numbered ball that is not a legal object ball, the impeding ball moves (regardless of whether it was moved by a hand, cue stick follow-through or bridge).

Legal Break Shot. (Defined) To execute a legal break, the breaker (with the cue ball behind the head string) must either (1) pocket a ball, or (2) drive at least four numbered balls to the rail. If he fails to make a legal break, it is a foul, and the incoming player has the option of (1) accepting the table in position and shooting, or (2) having the balls reracked and having the options of shooting the opening break himself or allowing the offending player to rebreak.

Scratch on a Legal Break. If a player scratches on a legal break shot, (1) all balls pocketed remain pocketed (exception, the 8-ball: see rule on ILLEGALLY POCKETED BALLS), (2) it is a foul, (3) the table is open. PLEASE NOTE: Incoming player has a cue ball in hand behind the head string and may not shoot an object ball that is behind the head string, unless he first shoots the cue ball past the head string and causes the cue ball to come back behind the head string and hit the object ball.

Object Balls Jumped Off the Table on the Break. If a player jumps an object ball off the table on the break shot, it is a foul and the incoming player has the option of (1) accepting the table in position and shooting, or (2) taking cue ball in hand behind the head string and shooting.

8-Ball Pocketed on the Break. If the 8-ball is pocketed on the break, the breaker may ask for re-rack or have the 8-ball spotted and continue shooting. If the breaker scratches while pocketing the 8-ball on the break, the incoming player has the option of a rerack or having the 8-ball spotted and begin shooting with ball in hand behind the head string.

Open Table. (Defined) The table is "open" when the choice of groups (stripes or solids) has not yet been determined. When the table is open, it is legal to hit a solid first to make a stripe or vice-versa. NOTE: The table is always open immediately after the break shot. When the table is open it is legal to hit any solid or stripe or the 8-ball first in the process of pocketing the called stripe or solid. However, when the table is open and the 8-ball is the first ball contacted, no stripe or solid may be scored in favor of the shooter. The shooter loses his turn; any balls pocketed remain pocketed; and the incoming player addresses the balls with the table still open. On an open table, all illegally pocketed balls remain pocketed.

Choice of Group. The choice of stripes or solids is not determined on the break even if balls are made from only one or both groups. THE TABLE IS ALWAYS OPEN IMMEDIATELY AFTER THE BREAK SHOT.

The choice of group is determined only when a player legally pockets a called object ball after the break shot.

Legal Shot.   (Defined) On all shots (except on the break and when the table is open), the shooter must hit one of his group of balls first and (1) pocket a numbered ball, or (2) cause the cue ball or any numbered ball to contact a rail. PLEASE NOTE: It is permissible for the shooter to bank the cue ball off a rail before contacting his object ball; however, after contact with his object ball, an object ball must be pocketed, OR the cue ball or any numbered ball must contact a rail. Failure to meet these requirements is a foul.

"Safety" Shot.   For tactical reasons a player may choose to pocket an obvious object ball and also discontinue his turn at the table by declaring "safety" in advance. A safety shot is defined as a legal shot. If the shooting player intends to play safe by pocketing an obvious object ball, then prior to the shot, he must declare a "safety" to his opponent. If this is NOT done, and one of the shooter's object balls is pocketed, the shooter will be required to shoot again. Any ball pocketed on a safety shot remains pocketed.

Scoring.   A player is entitled to continue shooting until he fails to legally pocket a ball of his group. After a player has legally pocketed all of this group of balls, he shoots to pocket the 8-ball.

Foul Penalty.   Opposing player gets cue ball in hand. This means that the player can place the cue ball anywhere on the table (does not have to be behind the head string except on opening break). This rule prevents a player from making intentional fouls which would put his opponent at a disadvantage. With "cue ball in hand," the player may use his hand or any part of his cue (including the tip) to position the cue ball. When placing the cue ball in position, any forward stroke motion contacting the cue ball will be a foul, if not a legal shot.

Combination Shots.   Combination shots are allowed; however, the 8-ball cannot be used as a first ball in the combination except when the table is open.

Illegally Pocketed Balls. An object ball is considered to be illegally pocketed when (1) that object ball is pocketed on the same shot a foul is committed, or (2) the called ball did not go in the designated pocket, or (3) a safety is called prior to the shot. Illegally pocketed balls remain pocketed.

Object Balls Jumped Off the Table. If any object ball is jumped off the table, it is a foul and loss of turn, unless it is the 8-ball, which is a loss of game. Any jumped object balls are spotted in numerical order according to General Rules for spotting balls.

Playing the 8-Ball. When shooting at the 8-ball, a scratch or foul is not loss of game if the 8-ball is not pocketed or jumped from the table. Incoming player has cue ball in hand.

Loss of Game. A player loses the game if he commits any of the following infractions:

a.   Fouls when pocketing the 8-ball (exception: see 8-BALL POCKETED ON THE BREAK).

b.   Pockets the 8-ball on the same stroke as the last of his group of balls.

c.   Jumps the 8-ball off the table at any time.

d.   Pockets the 8-ball in a pocket other than the one designated.

e.   Pockets the 8-ball when it is not the legal object ball.

NOTE: All infractions must be called before another shot is taken, or else it will be deemed that no infraction occurred.

Stalemated Game. If, after 3 consecutive turns at the table by each player (6 turns total), both players agree that attempting to pocket or move an object ball will result in loss of game, the balls will be reracked with the original breaker of the stalemated game breaking again. The stalemate rule may only be used when there are only two object balls and the 8-ball remaining on the table. PLEASE NOTE: Three consecutive fouls by one player is not a loss of game.

NINE BALL

PROFESSIONAL AND WORLD RULES

Except when clearly contradicted by these additional rules, the General Rules of Pocket Billiards apply.

Object of the Game.   Nine Ball is played with nine object balls numbered 1 through 9 and a cue ball. On each shot the first ball the cue ball contacts must be the lowest-numbered ball on the table, but the balls need not be pocketed in order. If a player pockets any ball on a legal shot, he remains at the table for another shot, and continues until he misses, fouls, or wins the game by pocketing the 9-ball. After a miss, the incoming player must shoot from the position left by the previous player, but after any foul the incoming player may start with the cue ball anywhere on the table. Players are not required to call any shot. A match ends when one of the players has won the required number of games.

Racking the Balls.   The object balls are racked in a diamond shape, with the 1-ball at the top of the diamond and on the foot spot, the 9-ball in the center of the diamond, and the other balls in random order, racked as tightly as possible. The game begins with cue ball in hand behind the head string.

Legal Break Shot.   The rules governing the break shot are the same as for other shots except:

a.   The breaker must strike the 1-ball first and either pocket a ball or drive at least four numbered balls to the rail.

b.   If the cue ball is pocketed or driven off the table, or the requirements of the opening break are not met, it is a foul, and the incoming player has cue ball in hand anywhere on the table.

c.   If on the break shot, the breaker causes an object ball to jump off the table, it is a foul and the incoming player has cue ball in hand anywhere on the table. The object ball is not respotted (exception: if the object ball is the 9-ball, it is respotted).

Continuing Play. On the shot immediately following a legal break, the shooter may play a "push out." (See Rule for PUSH OUT). If the breaker pockets one or more balls on a legal break, he continues to shoot until he misses, fouls, or wins the game. If the player misses or fouls, the other player begins his inning and shoots until he misses, fouls, or wins. The game ends when the 9-ball is pocketed on a legal shot, or the game is forfeited for a serious infraction of the rules.

Push Out. The player who shoots the shot immediately after a legal break may play a push out in an attempt to move the cue ball into a better position for the option that follows. On a push out, the cue ball is not required to contact any object ball nor any rail, but all other foul rules still apply. The player must announce his intention of playing a push out before the shot, or the shot is considered to be a normal shot. Any ball pocketed on a push out does not count and remains pocketed except the 9-ball. Following a legal push out, the incoming player is permitted to shoot from that position or to pass the shot back to the player who pushed out. A push out is not considered to be a foul as long as no rule (except rules for BAD HIT and NO RAIL) is violated. An illegal push out is penalized according to the type of foul committed. After a player scratches on the break shot, the incoming player cannot play a push out.

Fouls. When a player commits a foul, he must relinquish his run at the table and no balls pocketed on the foul shot are respotted (exception: if a pocketed ball is the 9-ball, it is respotted). The incoming player is awarded ball in hand; prior to his first shot he may place the cue ball anywhere on the table. If a player commits several fouls on one shot, they are counted as only one foul.

Bad Hit. If the first object ball contacted by the cue ball is not the lowest-numbered ball on the table, the shot is foul.

No Rail. If no object ball is pocketed, failure to drive the cue ball or any numbered ball to a rail after the cue ball contacts the object ball on is a foul.

In Hand. When the cue ball is in hand, the player may place the cue ball anywhere on the bed of the table, except in contact with an object ball. He may continue to adjust the position of the cue ball until he takes a shot.

Object Balls Jumped Off the Table.   An unpocketed ball is considered to be driven off the table if it comes to rest other than on the bed of the table. It is a foul to drive an object ball off the table. The jumped object ball(s) is not respotted (exception: if the object ball is the 9-ball, it is respotted) and play continues.

Jump and Massé Shot Foul.   If a match is not refereed, it will be considered a cue ball foul if during an attempt to jump, curve, or massé the cue ball over or around an impeding numbered ball, the impeding ball moves (regardless of whether it was moved by hand, cue stick follow-through or bridge).

Three Consecutive Fouls.   If a player fouls three consecutive times on three successive shots without making an intervening legal shot, he loses the game. The three fouls must occur in one game. The warning must be given between the second and third fouls.

A player's inning begins when it is legal for him to take a shot and ends at the end of a shot on which he misses, fouls or wins, or when he fouls between shots.

End of Game.   A game starts as soon as the cue ball crosses over the head string on the opening break. The 1-ball must be legally contacted on the break shot. The game ends at the end of a legal shot which pockets the 9-ball; or then a player forfeits the game as the result of a foul.

STRAIGHT

PROFESSIONAL AND WORLD RULES

Except when clearly contradicted by these additional rules, the General Rules of Pocket Billiards apply.

Object of the Game.   Straight is a nomination game. The player must nominate a ball and a pocket. The player is awarded one point for every correctly nominated and pocketed ball on a legal stroke, and is allowed to continue his turn until he either fails to pocket a nominated ball or commits a foul. The player can pocket the first 14 balls, but before he can continue his turn by shooting at the 15th (and last remaining) ball on the table, the 14 pocketed balls are racked as before, except with the apex space (the space over the foot spot) vacant. The player then attempts to pocket the 15th ball in a manner so that the racked balls are disturbed and he can continue his run.

The player who scores the predetermined point total for a game (usually 150 in major tournament play or any agreed-upon total in casual play) prior to his opponent, wins the game.

Players.   2, or 2 teams.

Balls Used.   Standard set of object balls numbered 1-15, plus cue ball.

The Rack.   Standard triangle rack with the apex ball on the foot spot, 1-ball on the racker's right corner, 5-ball on the left corner. Other balls are placed at random and must touch their neighbors.

Scoring.   Any ball legally pocketed counts one point for the shooter.

Opening Break.   Starting player must either (1) designate a ball and a pocket into which that ball will be pocketed and accomplish the shot, or (2) cause the cue ball to contact a ball and then a cushion, plus cause two object balls to contact a cushion. Failure to meet at least one of the above requirements is a breaking violation. Offender's score is assessed a two-point penalty for each breaking violation. In addition, the opponent has the choice of (1) accepting the table in position, or (2) having the balls reracked and requiring the offending player to repeat the opening break. That choice continues until the opening break is not a breaking violation, or until the opponent accepts the table in position. The three successive fouls rule does not apply to breaking violations.

If the starting player scratches on a legal opening break, he is charged with a foul and assessed a one-point penalty, which applies toward the "Successive Fouls Penalties." The incoming player is awarded cue ball in hand behind the head string, with object balls in position.

Rules of Play.

1. A legally pocketed ball entitles a shooter to continue at the table until he fails to legally pocket a called ball on a shot. A player may not shoot any ball he chooses, but before he shoots, must designate the called ball and called pocket. He need not indicate any detail such as kisses, caroms, combinations, or cushions (all of which are legal). Any additionally pocketed ball(s) on a legal stroke is scored as one point for the shooter.

2. On all shots, a player must cause the cue ball to contact an object ball and then (1) pocket a numbered ball, or (2) cause the cue ball or any numbered ball to contact a cushion. Failure to meet these requirements is a foul.

When an object ball is not frozen to a cushion, but is within a ball's width of a cushion (referee to determine by measurement if necessary), a player is permitted only two consecutive legal safeties on that ball using only the near rail. If such safety is employed, that object ball is then considered frozen to the rail on the player's next inning. The General Rules of Pocket Billiards "Frozen Balls" requirements apply if the player chooses to make his first cue ball contact with that object ball on his third shot.

(NOTE: If a player has committed a foul on the shot immediately before or the shot immediately after playing this ball, then he must immediately meet the requirements of the "Frozen Ball" rule when playing this object ball. If such player fails to meet the requirements of the "Frozen Ball" rule, he is considered to have committed a third successive foul and the appropriate point penalty is assessed as well as one point for each of the previous fouls. All fifteen balls are then reracked and the player committing the infraction is required to break as at the beginning of the game.)

3. When the fourteenth ball of a rack is pocketed, play stops momentarily with the fifteenth ball remaining in position on the table; the fourteen pocketed balls are then racked (with the space at the foot spot vacant in the triangle). Player then continues, normally pocketing the fifteenth (or "break" ball) in such manner as to have the cue ball carom into the rack and spread the balls to facilitate the continuance of his run. However, player is not compelled to shoot the fifteenth ball; he may shoot any ball he desires.

See diagram below on What To Do If the fifteenth ball is pocketed on the same stroke as the fourteenth ball.

4. A player may call a safety rather than an object ball (for defensive purposes). Safety play is legal, but must comply with all applicable rules. Player's inning ends when a safety is played, and pocketed balls are not scored. Any object ball pocketed on a call safety is spotted.

5. A player may not catch, touch, or in any way interfere with a ball as it travels toward a pocket or the rack area on a shot (to include catching a ball as it enters a pocket by having a hand in the pocket). If he does, he is charged with a special "deliberate foul" and is penalized one point for the foul and an additional fifteen-point penalty, for a total of sixteen points. The incoming player then has choice of (1) accepting the table in position with the cue ball in hand behind the head string, or (2) having all fifteen balls reracked and requiring the offending player to shoot under the requirements of the opening break.

6. If the fifteenth (unpocketed) ball of a rack and/or the cue ball interferes with the triangle being lowered straight down into position

What To Do If

15ᵗʰ BALL LIES \ CUE BALL LIES	IN THE RACK	NOT IN THE RACK AND NOT ON THE HEAD SPOT*	ON HEAD SPOT*
IN THE RACK	15ᵗʰ Ball: foot spot Cue Ball: in kitchen	15ᵗʰ Ball: head spot Cue Ball: in position	15ᵗʰ Ball: center spot Cue Ball: in position
POCKETED	15ᵗʰ Ball: foot spot Cue Ball: in kitchen	15ᵗʰ Ball: foot spot Cue Ball: in position	15ᵗʰ Ball: foot spot Cue Ball: in position
IN KITCHEN BUT NOT ON HEAD SPOT*	15ᵗʰ Ball: in position Cue Ball: head spot		
NOT IN KITCHEN AND NOT IN THE RACK	15ᵗʰ Ball: in position Cue Ball: in kitchen		
ON HEAD SPOT*	15ᵗʰ Ball: in position Cue Ball: center spot		

*Note: On head spot means to interfere with spotting a ball on the head spot.

for racking, refer to the diagram, which indicates the proper manner of relocating balls. (The lines out boxes are those situations in which there is no interference; both balls remain in position.)

7. When a player has the cue ball in hand behind the head string (as after a scratch) and all object balls are behind the head string, the object ball nearest the head string may be spotted at his request. If two or more balls are an equal distance from the head string, the player may designate which of the equidistant balls he desires to have spotted.

Illegally Pocketed Balls.   All spotted. No penalty.

Object Balls Jumped Off the Table.   The stroke is a foul. Any jumped ball(s) is spotted after the balls come to rest.

Cue Ball After Jumping Off the Table or Scratch.   Incoming player has cue ball in hand behind the head string, unless the rule SUCCESSIVE FOUL PENALTIES (below) applies to the offender's foul and dictate alternate choices or procedures.

Penalties for Fouls.   One point deducted for each foul. NOTE: more severe penalties for deliberate fouls (rule #5 under RULES OF PLAY) and third SUCCESSIVE FOULS (below). Incoming player accepts cue ball in position unless foul was a jumped cue ball, pocket scratch, deliberate foul or third successive foul.

Successive Foul Penalties.   When a player commits a foul, he is penalized one point (or more as appropriate) and a notation is made and posted by the scorer that he is "on a foul." The player remains "on a foul" until his next shot attempt, at which time he may remove the foul by successfully pocketing a called ball, or completing a legal safety. If he fails to meet these requirements on his next turn at the table, he is penalized one point. The notation is changed to "on two fouls." If he fails to meet the requirements of successfully pocketing a called ball or completing a legal safety on his third consecutive turn at the table, a penalty of fifteen points is assessed.

The commission of a third successive foul automatically clears the offender's record of fouls.

All balls are then reracked and the player committing the infraction is required to break as at the beginning of the game. Rules for the opening break apply.

It should be emphasized that successive fouls must be committed in successive turns (or playing attempts), not merely in successive innings. For example, if a player ends inning 6 with a foul, steps to the table for inning 7 and fouls (he is "on two fouls"), and then starts inning 8 with a legally pocketed ball before scratching on his second shot attempt of the inning, he has not committed three successive fouls, even though there were fouls in three successive innings. As soon as he legally pocketed the ball to start inning 8, he cleared the two fouls. He is, of course, "on one foul" when he plays the first stroke attempt of inning 9.

Scoring Note.   The deduction of penalty points can result in negative scores. A running score can read "minus one," "minus two," "minus fifteen," etc. (A player can win a game with a score of 150 while his opponent has scored but two fouls. The final score would read 150 to –2.)

If a player fouls on a shot that has not pocketed a ball, the point penalty is deducted from his score at the end of the previous inning. If a player fouls and pockets a ball on the same shot, that ball is spotted (not scored) and the point penalty is deducted from his score at the end of the previous inning.